Survival Communications in Delaware

DECEMBER 7, 1787

John E. Parnell, KK4HWX

13 – ISBN 978-1478191605
10 – ISBN 1478191600

Cover design by:
Lynda Colón
FREELANCE GRAPHIC DESIGN &
MARKETING COMMUNICATIONS
www.hirelynda.webs.com

Titles available in this series:

Survival Communications in Alabama
Survival Communications in Alaska
Survival Communications in Arizona
Survival Communications in Arkansas
Survival Communications in California
Survival Communications in Colorado
Survival Communications in Connecticut
Survival Communications in Delaware
Survival Communications in Florida
Survival Communications in Georgia
Survival Communications in Hawaii
Survival Communications in Idaho
Survival Communications in Illinois
Survival Communications in Indiana
Survival Communications in Iowa
Survival Communications in Kansas
Survival Communications in Kentucky
Survival Communications in Louisiana
Survival Communications in Maine
Survival Communications in Maryland
Survival Communications in Massachusetts
Survival Communications in Michigan
Survival Communications in Minnesota
Survival Communications in Mississippi
Survival Communications in Missouri

Survival Communications in Montana
Survival Communications in Nebraska
Survival Communications in Nevada
Survival Communications in New Hampshire
Survival Communications in New Jersey
Survival Communications in New Mexico
Survival Communications in New York
Survival Communications in North Carolina
Survival Communications in North Dakota
Survival Communications in Ohio
Survival Communications in Oklahoma
Survival Communications in Oregon
Survival Communications in Pennsylvania
Survival Communications in Rhode Island
Survival Communications in South Carolina
Survival Communications in South Dakota
Survival Communications in Tennessee
Survival Communications in Texas
Survival Communications in Utah
Survival Communications in Vermont
Survival Communications in Virginia
Survival Communications in Washington
Survival Communications in West Virginia
Survival Communications in Wisconsin
Survival Communications in Wyoming

The above titles are available from your favorite online or brick-and-mortar bookstore or directly from the publisher at Tutor Turtle Press LLC, 1027 S. Pendleton St. – Suite B-10, Easley, SC 29642 or on our website: www.TutorTurtlePress.com.

TABLE OF CONTENTS

Appendix A – Delaware Ham Radio Clubs

ARRL Affiliated Radio Clubs in Delaware – By City

Appendix B – FCC Amateur Radio Licenses in Delaware by City

Survival Communications in Delaware

Perhaps you have prepared for WTSHTF or TEOTWAWKI with respect to food, water, self-defense and shelter. But what about communication?

Whenever there is a disaster (hurricane, earthquake, economic collapse, nuclear war, EMF, solar eruption, etc.), the normal means of communication that we're all reliant upon (cell phone, land line phone, the Internet, etc.) will probably be, at best, sporadic and at worst, non-existent.

As this author sees it, short of smoke signals and mirrors, there are three options for communication in "trying times": (1) GMRS or FRS radios; (2) CB radios; and (3) ham or amateur radio. Let's consider each of these options to come up with the most acceptable one.

GMRS (General Mobile Radio Service) / FRS (Family Radio Service)

GMRS (General Mobile Radio Service) / FRS (Family Radio Service) radios work optimally over short distances where there is minimal interference. Originally designed to be used as pagers, particularly inside a building or other such confined area, these radios are low-cost and convenient to carry. Unfortunately their small size and light weight comes with a trade-off – short range and short battery life. These radios are supposed to be able to communicate for up to 25-30 miles. Right. That's on level terrain, without buildings or trees getting in the way. While battery life technology is constantly improving, you will need spare batteries to keep communicating or someway of recharging the ones in the radio. In this author's opinion, GMRS/FRS radios are not first choice when concerned with medium or long range communication.

CB (Citizens Band)

CB (Citizens Band) radios operate in a frequency range originally reserved for ham or amateur radio operation. Because of the overwhelming number of people wishing quick, low-cost, regulation-free communication, the FCC (Federal Communication Commission) split off a portion of the frequency spectrum and allowed anyone to purchase a CB radio and start communicating. No test. No license. Just personal/business communication. Today, CB radios are readily available in such outlets as eBay and Craigslist. This author has seen them at yard/garage/tag sales and at flea markets.

CB radios come in a variety of "flavors." Fixed units, sometimes referred to as base units are intended for home use. For the most part, they derive their power from the utility company. In the event of loss of electricity, most base units can also be connected to a 12-volt battery, like that in your car/truck. If you choose to obtain a fixed unit, make sure you know how to connect the unit to the battery – ahead of time. Trying to figure this out when you're under extra stress is not a good situation.

A second type of CB radio is designed to be mobile, that is, installed in your car/truck. It gets its power from the vehicle's battery. You can either attach an antenna permanently to the vehicle or have a removable, magnetic type antenna.

The third type of CB radio is designed for handheld use. They are small and light. Most weigh less than a pound and operate on batteries. Yes, using batteries in a CB poses the same limitations as those by the GMRS/FRS radios, but have the added advantage that most handheld units come with a cigarette lighter adapter. Comes in handy when you are on the move and wish to be able to communicate both from a vehicle and also when you have to abandon it.

While they have a greater range than GMRS/FRS radios, CB radios are, legally, limited to operate on 40 channels, with a power rating of four (4) watts or less. Yes, it is possible to alter CB radios to get around these limitations, but not legally,

Ham/Amateur Radio

Ham/Amateur radio is very appealing. With a ham radio, you are not limited to less than 50 miles, but can communicate with anyone in the world (who also has access to a ham radio, of course).

Standardized Amateur Radio Prepper Communications Plan

In the event of a nationwide catastrophic disaster, the nationwide network of Amateur Radio licensed preppers will need a set of standardized meeting frequencies to share information and coordinate activities between various prepper groups. This Standardized Amateur Radio Communications Plan establishes a set of frequencies on the 80 meter, 40 meter, 20 meter, and 2 meter Amateur Radio bands for use during these types of catastrophic disasters.

Routine nets will not be held on all of these frequencies, but preppers are encouraged to use them when coordinating with other preppers on a routine basis. Routine nets may be conducted by The American Preparedness Radio Net (TAPRN) on these or other frequencies as they see fit. However, TAPRN will promote the use of these standardized frequencies by all Amateur Radio licensed preppers during times of catastrophic disaster. The promotion of this Standardized Amateur Radio Communications Plan is encouraged by all means within the prepper community, including via Amateur Radio, Twitter, Facebook, and various blogs.

Standardized Frequencies and Modes
80 Meters – 3.818 MHz LSB (TAPRN Net: Sundays at 9 PM ET)   40 Meters – 7.242 MHz LSB   40 Meters Morse Code / Digital – 7.073 MHz USB (TAPRN: Sundays at 7:30 PM ET on   CONTESTIA 4/250)   20 Meters – 14.242 MHz USB   2 Meters – 146.420 MHz FM

Nets and Network Etiquette

In times of nationwide catastrophic disaster, the ability of any one prepper to initiate and sustain themselves as a net control may be limited by the availability of power and other resource shortages. However, all licensed preppers are encouraged to maintain a listening watch on these frequencies as often as possible during a catastrophic disaster. Preppers may routinely announce themselves in the following manner:

• This is [Your Callsign Phonetically] in [Your State], maintaining a listening watch on [Standard Frequency] for any preppers on frequency seeking information or looking to provide information. Please call [Your Callsign Phonetically]. Preppers exchanging information that may require follow up should agree upon a designated time to return to the frequency and provide further information. If other stations are utilizing the frequency at the designated time you return, maintain watch and proceed with your communications when those stations are finished. If your communications are urgent and the stations on frequency are not passing information of a critical nature, interrupt with the word "Break" and request use of the frequency.

For More Information

Catastrophe Network: http://www.catastrophenetwork.org or @CatastropheNet on Twitter The American Preparedness Radio Network: http://www.taprn.com or @TAPRN on Twitter

© 2011 Catastrophe Network, Please Distribute Freely

In order to use a ham radio, legally, one must be licensed to do so by the FCC (other countries have analogous governmental bodies to regulate ham radio). To obtain a license is quite easy – take a test and pay your license fee. There are currently three classes of license – Technician, General, and Amateur Extra. With each of these licenses come specific abilities.

Technician class is the beginning level. The exam consists of 35 multiple choice questions randomly drawn from a pool of 395 questions. The question pool is readily available online for free downloading (http://www.ncvec.org/downloads/Revised%20Element%202.Pdf) or in such publications at *Ham Radio License Manual Revised 2nd Edition* (ISBN 978-0-87259-097-7). The current Technician pool of questions is to be used from July 1, 2010 to June 30, 2014. Be sure the question pool you are studying from is current. You will need to score at least 26 correct to pass. (Do not worry, Morse Code is no longer on the test, although many ham operators use it anyway.) You do not need to take a formal class in order to qualify to take the exam. You can learn the material on your own. Most people spend 10-15 hours studying and then successfully take the exam. The cost of taking the exam is under $20. The exam is given in MANY locations throughout the US. Usually the exam is given by area ham clubs. You do not have to belong to the club to take the exam. Check Appendix A for a listing of clubs in Delaware.

Topics for the Technician License in Amateur Radio

The Technician license exam covers such topics as basic regulations, operating practices, and electronic theory, with a focus on VHF and UHF applications. Below is the syllabus for the Technician Class.

Subelement T1 – FCC Rules, descriptions and definitions for the amateur radio service, operator and station license responsibilities

[6 Exam Questions – 6 Groups]

T1A – Amateur Radio services; purpose of the amateur service, amateur-satellite service, operator/primary station license grant, where FCC rules are codified, basis and purpose of FCC rules, meanings of basic terms used in FCC rules

T1B – Authorized frequencies; frequency allocations, ITU regions, emission type, restricted sub-bands, spectrum sharing, transmissions near band edges

T1C – Operator classes and station call signs; operator classes, sequential, special event, and vanity call sign systems, international communications, reciprocal operation, station license licensee, places where the amateur service is regulated by the FCC, name and address on ULS, license term, renewal, grace period

T1D – Authorized and prohibited transmissions

T1E – Control operator and control types; control operator required, eligibility, designation of control operator, privileges and duties, control point, local, automatic and remote control, location of control operator

T1F – Station identification and operation standards; special operations for repeaters and auxiliary stations, third party communications, club stations, station security, FCC inspection

Subelement T2 – Operating Procedures

[3 Exam Questions – 3 Groups]

T2A – Station operation; choosing an operating frequency, calling another station, test transmissions, use of minimum power, frequency use, band plans

T2B – VHF/UHF operating practices; SSB phone, FM repeater, simplex, frequency offsets, splits and shifts, CTCSS, DTMF, tone squelch, carrier squelch, phonetics

T2C – Public service; emergency and non-emergency operations, message traffic handling

Subelement T3 – Radio wave characteristics, radio and electromagnetic properties, propagation modes

[3 Exam Questions – 3 Groups]

T3A – Radio wave characteristics; how a radio signal travels; distinctions of HF, VHF and UHF; fading, multipath; wavelength vs. penetration; antenna orientation

T3B – Radio and electromagnetic wave properties; the electromagnetic spectrum, wavelength vs. frequency, velocity of electromagnetic waves

T3C – Propagation modes; line of sight, sporadic E, meteor, aurora scatter, tropospheric ducting, F layer skip, radio horizon

Subelement T4 - Amateur radio practices and station setup

[2 Exam Questions – 2 Groups]

T4A – Station setup; microphone, speaker, headphones, filters, power source, connecting a computer, RF grounding

T4B – Operating controls; tuning, use of filters, squelch, AGC, repeater offset, memory channels

Subelement T5 – Electrical principles, math for electronics, electronic principles, Ohm's Law

[4 Exam Questions – 4 Groups]

T5A – Electrical principles; current and voltage, conductors and insulators, alternating and direct current

T5B – Math for electronics; decibels, electronic units and the metric system

T5C – Electronic principles; capacitance, inductance, current flow in circuits, alternating current, definition of RF, power calculations

T5D – Ohm's Law

Subelement T6 – Electrical components, semiconductors, circuit diagrams, component functions

[4 Exam Groups – 4 Questions]

T6A – Electrical components; fixed and variable resistors, capacitors, and inductors; fuses, switches, batteries

T6B – Semiconductors; basic principles of diodes and transistors

T6C – Circuit diagrams; schematic symbols

T6D – Component functions

Subelement T7 – Station equipment, common transmitter and receiver problems, antenna measurements and troubleshooting, basic repair and testing

[4 Exam Questions – 4 Groups]

T7A – Station radios; receivers, transmitters, transceivers

T7B – Common transmitter and receiver problems; symptoms of overload and overdrive, distortion, interference, over and under modulation, RF feedback, off frequency signals; fading and noise; problems with digital communications interfaces

T7C – Antenna measurements and troubleshooting; measuring SWR, dummy loads, feedline failure modes

T7D – Basic repair and testing; soldering, use of a voltmeter, ammeter, and ohmmeter

Subelement T8 – Modulation modes, amateur satellite operation, operating activities, non-voice communications

[4 Exam Questions – 4 Groups]

T8A – Modulation modes; bandwidth of various signals

T8B – Amateur satellite operation; Doppler shift, basic orbits, operating protocols

T8C – Operating activities; radio direction finding, radio control, contests, special event stations, basic linking over Internet

T8D – Non-voice communications; image data, digital modes, CW, packet, PSK31

Subelement T9 – Antennas, feedlines

[2 Exam Groups – 2 Questions]

T9A – Antennas; vertical and horizontal, concept of gain, common portable and mobile antennas, relationships between antenna length and frequency

T9B – Feedlines; types, losses vs. frequency, SWR concepts, matching, weather protection, connectors

Subelement T0 – AC power circuits, antenna installation, RF hazards

[3 Exam Questions – 3 Groups]

T0A – AC power circuits; hazardous voltages, fuses and circuit breakers, grounding, lightning protection, battery safety, electrical code compliance

T0B – Antenna installation; tower safety, overhead power lines

T0C – RF hazards; radiation exposure, proximity to antennas, recognized safe power levels, exposure to others

Once your name and call sign are available in the FCC database, you have the privilege of operating on all VHF (2 m) and UHF (70 cm) frequencies above 30 megahertz (MHz) and HF frequencies 80, 40, and 15 meter, and on the 10 meter band using Morse code (CW), voice, and digital mode. For a Technician license in Delaware, your call sign will consist of a two-letter prefix beginning with K or W, the number three (3), and a three-letter suffix. The single digit number in the call sign is determined according to which area of the US you obtain your first license. Even though you may move to another state, you keep this number in your call sign. This is also true should you upgrade to a higher license and get a new call sign. The numeral portion of your call sign stays the same.

Call Sign Numbers

Below is a chart showing the various numbers and the state(s) in which you would obtain the number.

Call Sign Number	State(s)
0	CO, IA, KS, MN, MO, NE, ND, SD
1	CT, ME, MA, NH, RI, VT
2	NJ, NY
3	DE, DC, MD, PA
4	AL, FL, GA, KY, NC, SC, TN, VA
5	AR, LA, MS, NM, OK, TX
6	CA
7	AZ, ID, MT, NV, OR, WA, UT, WY
8	MI, OH, WV
9	IL, IN, WI

Residents of Alaska may have any of the following call sign prefixes assigned to them: AL0-7, KL0-7, NL0-7, or WL0-7. Likewise, residents of Hawaii may have the prefix AH6-7, KH6-7, NH6-7, or WH6-7 assigned.

Once you obtain your Technician license, do not stop there. Go and get your General license.

General is the second of three ham license classes. Like the Technician license, to get a General license, you merely have to take a 35-question multiple choice exam and pay your license fee. Passing is still at least 26 correct answers and the fee is the same (less than $20). Again the question pool is available for free online (http://www.ncvec.org/page.php?id=358). It is also available in such print publications as *The ARRL General Class License Manual 7*[th] *Edition* (ISBN 978-0-87259-811-9). The current General pool of questions is to be used from July 1, 2011 to June 30, 2015. Be sure the question pool you are using is current. Being a bit more comprehensive than the Technician license, the General license usually requires 15-20 hours of study to learn the material. Check Appendix A for a listing of clubs in Delaware where you might take your exam. Once your name and NEW call sign is listed in the FCC database, you're good to go. For a General license in Delaware, your call sign will consist of a one-letter prefix beginning with K, N or W, the number three (3), and a three-letter suffix.

Topics for the General License in Amateur Radio

The General license exam covers regulations, operating practices and electronic theory. Below is the syllabus for the General Class.

Subelement G1 – Commission's Rules
(5 Exam Questions – 5 Groups)
G1A – General Class control operator frequency privileges; primary and secondary allocations
G1B – Antenna structure limitations; good engineering and good amateur practice, beacon operation; restricted operation; retransmitting radio signals
G1C – Transmitter power regulations; data emission standards
G1D – Volunteer Examiners and Volunteer Examiner Coordinators; temporary identification
G1E – Control categories; repeater regulations; harmful interference; third party rules; ITU regions

Subelement G2 – Operating procedures
(5 Exam Questions – 5 Groups)
G2A – Phone operating procedures; USB/LSB utilization conventions; procedural signals; breaking into a OSO in progress; VOX operation
G2B – Operating courtesy; band plans, emergencies, including drills and emergency communications
G2C – CW operating procedures and procedural signals; Q signals and common abbreviations; full break in
G2D – Amateur Auxiliary; minimizing interference; HF operations

G2E – Digital operating; procedures, procedural signals and common abbreviations

Subelement G3 – Radio wave propagation

(3 Exam Questions – 3 Groups)

G3A – Sunspots and solar radiation; ionospheric disturbances; propagation forecasting and indices

G3B – Maximum Usable Frequency; Lowest Usable Frequency; propagation

G3C – Ionospheric layers; critical angle and frequency; HF scatter; Near Vertical Incidence Sky waves

Subelement G4 – Amateur radio practices

(5 Exam Questions – 5 Groups)

G4A – Station Operation and setup

G4B – Test and monitoring equipment; two-tone test

G4C – Interference with consumer electronics; grounding; DSP

G4D – Speech processors; S meters; sideband operation near band edges

G4E – HF mobile radio installations; emergency and battery powered operation

Subelement G5 – Electrical principles

(3 Exam Questions – 3 Groups)

G5A – Reactance; inductance; capacitance; impedance; impedance matching

G5B – The Decibel; current and voltage dividers; electrical power calculations; sine wave root-mean-square (RMS) values; PEP calculations

G5C – Resistors; capacitors and inductors in series and parallel; transformers

Subelement G6 – Circuit components

(3 Exam Questions – 3 Groups)

G6A – Resistors; capacitors; inductors

G6B – Rectifiers; solid state diodes and transistors; vacuum tubes; batteries

G6C – Analog and digital integrated circuits (ICs); microprocessors; memory; I/O devices; microwave ICs (MMICs); display devices

Subelement G7 – Practical circuits

(3 Exam Questions – 3 Groups)

G7A – Power supplies; schematic symbols

G7B – Digital circuits; amplifiers and oscillators

G7C – Receivers and transmitters; filters, oscillators

Subelement G8 – Signals and emissions

(2 Exam Questions – 2 Groups)

> G8A – Carriers and modulation; AM; FM; single and double sideband; modulation envelope; overmodulation
>
> G8B – Frequency mixing; multiplication; HF data communications; bandwidths of various modes; deviation

Subelement G9 – Antennas and feed lines

(4 Exam Questions – 4 Groups)
G9A – Antenna feed lines; characteristic impedance and attenuation; SWR calculation, measurement and effects; matching networks
G9B – Basic antennas
G9C – Directional antennas
G9D – Specialized antennas

Subelement G0 – Electrical and RF safety

(2 Exam Questions – 2 Groups)
G0A – RF safety principles, rules and guidelines; routine station elevation
G0B – Safety in the ham shack; electrical shock and treatment, safety grounding, fusing, interlocks, wiring, antenna and tower safety

With a General license, you can use all VHF and UHF frequencies and most of the HF frequencies. You would have access to the 160, 30, 17, 12, and 10 meter bands and access to major parts of the 80, 40, 20, and 15 meter bands. Of course, this is in addition to all bands available to Technician license holders.

Amateur Extra is the third of three ham license classes. Like the Technician and General classes, you merely have to pass a test and pay your fee to get your Amateur Extra license. This class of license is more comprehensive than the lower license classes. The exam is longer – 50 questions – and the minimum passing score is higher – 37. However, once you get your Amateur Extra license, all ham frequencies, VHF, UHF and HF are available for your enjoyment. The Extra exam covers regulations, specialized operating practices, advanced electronics theory, and radio equipment design.

Like for the other license classes, the question pool for the Amateur Extra license is available online for downloading (http://www.ncvec.org/downloads/REVISED%202012-2016%20Extra%20Class%20Pool.doc). It is also available in print form in such publications as *The ARRL Extra Class License Manual Revised 9th Edition* (ISBN 978-0-87259-887-4).

Topics for the Extra License in Amateur Radio

Below is the syllabus for the Amateur Extra Class for July 1, 2012 to June 30, 2016.

Subelement E1 – Commission's Rules

[6 Exam Questions – 6 Groups]
E1A – Operating Standards: frequency privileges; emission standards; automatic message forwarding; frequency sharing; stations aboard ships or aircraft

E1B – Station restrictions and special operations: restrictions on station location; general operating restrictions, spurious emissions, control operator reimbursement; antenna structure restrictions; RACES operations

E1C – Station control: definitions and restrictions pertaining to local, automatic and remote control operation; control operator responsibilities for remote and automatically controlled stations

E1D – Amateur Satellite service: definitions and purpose; license requirements for space stations; available frequencies and bands; telecommand and telemetry operations; restrictions, and special provisions; notification requirements

E1E – Volunteer examiner program: definitions, qualifications, preparation and administration of exams; accreditation; question pools; documentation requirements

E1F – Miscellaneous rules: external RF power amplifiers; national quiet zone; business communications; compensated communications; spread spectrum; auxiliary stations; reciprocal operating privileges; IARP and CEPT licenses; third party communications with foreign countries; special temporary authority

Subelement E2 – Operating procedures

[5 Exam Questions – 5 Groups]

E2A – Amateur radio in space: amateur satellites; orbital mechanics; frequencies and modes; satellite hardware; satellite operations

E2B – Television practices: fast scan television standards and techniques; slow scan television standards and techniques

E2C – Operating methods: contest and DX operating; spread-spectrum transmissions; selecting an operating frequency

E2D – Operating methods: VHF and UHF digital modes; APRS

E2E – Operating methods: operating HF digital modes; error correction

Subelement E3 – Radio wave propagation

[3 Exam Questions – 3 Groups]

E3A – Propagation and technique, Earth-Moon-Earth communications; meteor scatter

E3B – Propagation and technique, trans-equatorial; long path; gray-line; multi-path propagation

E3C – Propagation and technique, Aurora propagation; selective fading; radio-path horizon; take-off angle over flat or sloping terrain; effects of ground on propagation; less common propagation modes

Subelement E4 – Amateur practices

[5 Exam Questions – 5 Groups]

E4A – Test equipment: analog and digital instruments; spectrum and network analyzers, antenna analyzers; oscilloscopes; testing transistors; RF measurements

E4B – Measurement technique and limitations: instrument accuracy and performance limitations; probes; techniques to minimize errors; measurement of "Q"; instrument calibration

E4C – Receiver performance characteristics, phase noise, capture effect, noise floor, image rejection, MDS, signal-to-noise-ratio; selectivity

E4D – Receiver performance characteristics, blocking dynamic range, intermodulation and cross-modulation interference; 3rd order intercept; desensitization; preselection

E4E – Noise suppression: system noise; electrical appliance noise; line noise; locating noise sources; DSP noise reduction; noise blankers

Subelement E5 – Electrical principles

[4 Exam Questions – 4 Groups]

E5A – Resonance and Q: characteristics of resonant circuits: series and parallel resonance; Q; half-power bandwidth; phase relationships in reactive circuits

E5B – Time constants and phase relationships: RLC time constants: definition; time constants in RL and RC circuits; phase angle between voltage and current; phase angles of series and parallel circuits

E5C – Impedance plots and coordinate systems: plotting impedances in polar coordinates; rectangular coordinates

E5D – AC and RF energy in real circuits: skin effect; electrostatic and electromagnetic fields; reactive power; power factor; coordinate systems

Subelement E6 – Circuit components

[6 Exam Questions – 6 Groups]

E6A – Semiconductor materials and devices: semiconductor materials germanium, silicon, P-type, N-type; transistor types: NPN, PNP, junction, field-effect transistors: enhancement mode; depletion mode; MOS; CMOS; N-channel; P-channel

E6B – Semiconductor diodes

E6C – Integrated circuits: TTL digital integrated circuits; CMOS digital integrated circuits; gates

E6D – Optical devices and toroids: cathode-ray tube devices; charge-coupled devices (CCDs); liquid crystal displays (LCDs); toroids: permeability, core material, selecting, winding

E6E – Piezoelectric crystals and MMICs: quartz crystals; crystal oscillators and filters; monolithic amplifiers

E6F – Optical components and power systems: photoconductive principles and effects, photovoltaic systems, optical couplers, optical sensors, and optoisolators

Subelement E7 – Practical circuits

[8 Exam Questions – 8 Groups]

E7A – Digital circuits: digital circuit principles and logic circuits: classes of logic elements; positive and negative logic; frequency dividers; truth tables

E7B – Amplifiers: Class of operation; vacuum tube and solid-state circuits; distortion and intermodulation; spurious and parasitic suppression; microwave amplifiers

E7C – Filters and matching networks: filters and impedance matching networks: types of networks; types of filters; filter applications; filter characteristics; impedance matching; DSP filtering

E7D – Power supplies and voltage regulators

E7E – Modulation and demodulation: reactance, phase and balanced modulators; detectors; mixer stages; DSP modulation and demodulation; software defined radio systems

E7F – Frequency markers and counters: frequency divider circuits; frequency marker generators; frequency counters

E7G – Active filters and op-amps: active audio filters; characteristics; basic circuit design; operational amplifiers

E7H – Oscillators and signal sources: types of oscillators; synthesizers and phase-locked loops; direct digital synthesizers

Subelement E8 – Signals and emissions

[4 Exam Questions – 4 Groups]

E8A – AC waveforms: sine, square, sawtooth and irregular waveforms; AC measurements; average and PEP of RF signals; pulse and digital signal waveforms

E8B – Modulation and demodulation: modulation methods; modulation index and deviation ratio; pulse modulation; frequency and time division multiplexing

E8C – Digital signals: digital communications modes; CW; information rate vs. bandwidth; spread-spectrum communications; modulation methods

E8D – Waves, measurements, and RF grounding: peak-to-peak values, polarization; RF grounding

Subelement E9 – Antennas and transmission lines

[8 Exam Questions – 8 Groups]

E9A – Isotropic and gain antennas: definition; used as a standard for comparison; radiation pattern; basic antenna parameters: radiation resistance and reactance, gain, beamwidth, efficiency

E9B – Antenna patterns: E and H plane patterns; gain as a function of pattern; antenna design; Yagi antennas

E9C – Wire and phased vertical antennas: beverage antennas; terminated and resonant rhombic antennas; elevation above real ground; ground effects as related to polarization; take-off angles

E9D – Directional antennas: gain; satellite antennas; antenna beamwidth; losses; SWR bandwidth; antenna efficiency; shortened and mobile antennas; grounding

E9E – Matching: matching antennas to feed lines; power dividers

E9F – Transmission lines: characteristics of open and shorted feed lines: 1/8 wavelength; 1/4 wavelength; 1/2 wavelength; feed lines: coax versus open-wire; velocity factor; electrical length; transformation characteristics of line terminated in impedance not equal to characteristic impedance

E9G – The Smith chart

E9H – Effective radiated power; system gains and losses; radio direction finding antennas

Subelement E0 – Safety

[1 exam question – 1 group]

E0A – Safety: amateur radio safety practices; RF radiation hazards; hazardous materials

Once your new call sign is listed in the FCC database, you are good to go. For an Amateur Extra license in Delaware, your call sign will consist of a prefix of K, N or W, the number three (3), and a two-letter suffix, or a two-letter prefix beginning with A, N, K or W, the number three (3), and a one-letter suffix, or a two-letter prefix beginning with A, the number three (3), and a two-letter suffix.

Ham radio equipment can be expensive or you can do it "on the cheap." The cost will run from a couple hundred dollars to well in the thousands, depending on what you have available. eBay, and Craigslist are good places to start looking. Most ham clubs do some sort of hamfest annually wherein club members or others are willing to part with older equipment. See Appendix A for a list of clubs in Delaware.

Another excellent source of equipment, as well as advice on setting the equipment up and how to use it properly, is current ham operators. In Appendix B, the author has listed all the FCC licensed ham operators in Delaware, listed by city, and then sorted by street and house number on the street. Who knows, maybe someone who lives close to you is a ham operator. Be a good neighbor, stop by and have a chat with him/her.

Like CB radios, ham radios come in three formats – base, mobile, and handheld. They can use the electric company for power, or operate off a car battery. In the opinion of this author, in spite of the slightly higher cost of the equipment and having to take a test to legally use the equipment, ham radio is the way to go when concerned about communication during times of crisis.

Canadian Call Sign Prefixes

Because of our proximity to Canada, many times ham contact is made with our northern neighbors. Below is a chart showing the origin of Canadian call sign prefixes.

Call Sign Prefix	Provence or Territory
CY0	Sable Island
CY9	St. Paul Island
VA1, VE1	New Brunswick, Nova Scotia
VA2, VE2	Quebec
VA3, VE3	Ontario
VA4, VE4	Manitoba
VA5, VE5	Saskatchewan
VA6, VE6	Alberta
VA7, VE7	British Columbia
VE8	North West Territories
VE9	New Brunswick
VO1	Newfoundland
VO2	Labrador
VY0	Nunavut
VY1	Yukon
VY2	Prince Edward Island

Common Radio Bands in the United States

Certain radio bands are more popular with ham radio enthusiasts than others. Below is a chart showing these bands and when they are most popular.

	Band (meter)	Frequency (MHz)	Use
HF	160	1.8 – 2.0	Night
	80	3.5 – 4.0	Night and Local Day
	40	7.0 – 7.3	Night and Local Day
	30	10.1 – 10.15	CW and Digital
	20	14.0 – 14.350	World Wide Day and Night
	17	18.068 – 18.168	World Wide Day and Night
	15	21.0 – 21.450	Primarily Daytime
	12	24.890 – 24.990	Primarily Daytime
	10	28.0 – 29.70	Daytime during Sunspot highs
VHF	6	50 – 54	Local to World Wide
	2	144 – 148	Local to Medium Distance
UHF	70 cm	430 – 440	Local

Common Amateur Radio Bands in Canada

160 Meter Band - Maximum bandwidth 6 kHz
1.800 - 1.820 MHz - CW
1.820 - 1.830 MHz - Digital Modes
1 830 - 1.840 MHz - DX Window
1.840 - 2.000 MHz - SSB and other wide band modes

80 Meter Band - Maximum bandwidth 6 kHz
3.500 - 3.580 MHz - CW
3.580 - 3.620 MHz - Digital Modes
3.620 - 3.635 MHz - Packet/Digital Secondary
3.635 - 3.725 MHz - CW
3.725 - 3.790 MHz - SSB and other side band modes*
3.790 - 3.800 MHz - SSB DX Window
3.800 - 4.000 MHz - SSB and other wide band modes

40 Meter Band - Maximum bandwidth 6 kHz
7.000 - 7.035 MHz - CW
7.035 - 7.050 MHz - Digital Modes
7.040 - 7.050 MHz - International packet
7.050 - 7.100 MHz - SSB
7.100 - 7.120 MHz - Packet within Region 2
7.120 - 7.150 MHz - CW
7.150 - 7.300 MHz - SSB and other wide band modes

30 Meter Band - Maximum bandwidth 1 kHz

10.100 - 10.130 MHz - CW only
10.130 - 10.140 MHz - Digital Modes
10.140 - 10.150 MHz - Packet

20 Meter Band - Maximum bandwidth 6 kHz

14.000 - 14.070 MHz - CW only
14.070 - 14.095 MHz - Digital Mode
14.095 - 14.099 MHz - Packet
14.100 MHz - Beacons
14.101 - 14.112 MHz - CW, SSB, packet shared
14.112 - 14.350 MHz - SSB
14.225 - 14.235 MHz - SSTV

17 Meter Band - Maximum bandwidth 6 kHz

18.068 - 18.100 MHz - CW
18.100 - 18.105 MHz - Digital Modes
18.105 - 18.110 MHz - Packet
18.110 - 18.168 MHz - SSB and other wide band modes

15 Meter Band - maximum bandwidth 6 kHz

21.000 - 21.070 MHz - CW
21.070 - 21.090 MHz - Digital Modes
21.090 - 21.125 MHz - Packet
21.100 - 21.150 MHz - CW and SSB
21.150 - 21.335 MHz - SSB and other wide band modes
21.335 - 21.345 MHz - SSTV
21.345 - 21.450 MHz - SSB and other wide band modes

12 Meter Band - Maximum bandwidth 6 kHz

24.890 - 24.930 MHz - CW
24.920 - 24.925 MHz - Digital Modes
24.925 - 24.930 MHz - Packet
24.930 - 24.990 MHz - SSB and other wide band modes

10 Meter Band - Maximum band width 20 kHz

28.000 - 28.200 MHz - CW
28.070 - 28.120 MHz - Digital Modes
28.120 - 28.190 MHz - Packet
28.190 - 28.200 MHz - Beacons
28.200 - 29.300 MHz - SSB and other wide band modes
29.300 - 29.510 MHz - Satellite
29.510 - 29.700 MHz - SSB, FM and repeaters

160 Meters (1.8-2.0 MHz)

1.800 - 2.000 CW
1.800 - 1.810 Digital Modes
1.810 CW QRP
1.843-2.000 SSB, SSTV and other wideband modes
1.910 SSB QRP
1.995 - 2.000 Experimental
1.999 - 2.000 Beacons

80 Meters (3.5-4.0 MHz)

3.590 RTTY/Data DX
3.570-3.600 RTTY/Data
3.790-3.800 DX window
3.845 SSTV
3.885 AM calling frequency

40 Meters (7.0-7.3 MHz)

7.040 RTTY/Data DX
7.080-7.125 RTTY/Data
7.171 SSTV
7.290 AM calling frequency

30 Meters (10.1-10.15 MHz)

10.130-10.140 RTTY
10.140-10.150 Packet

20 Meters (14.0-14.35 MHz)

14.070-14.095 RTTY
14.095-14.0995 Packet
14.100 NCDXF Beacons
14.1005-14.112 Packet
14.230 SSTV
14.286 AM calling frequency

17 Meters (18.068-18.168 MHz)

18.100-18.105 RTTY
18.105-18.110 Packet

15 Meters (21.0-21.45 MHz)

21.070-21.110 RTTY/Data
21.340 SSTV

12 Meters (24.89-24.99 MHz)

24.920-24.925 RTTY
24.925-24.930 Packet

10 Meters (28-29.7 MHz)

28.000-28.070 CW
28.070-28.150 RTTY
28.150-28.190 CW
28.200-28.300 Beacons
28.300-29.300 Phone
28.680 SSTV
29.000-29.200 AM
29.300-29.510 Satellite Downlinks
29.520-29.590 Repeater Inputs
29.600 FM Simplex
29.610-29.700 Repeater Outputs

6 Meters (50-54 MHz)

50.0-50.1 CW, beacons
50.060-50.080 beacon subband
50.1-50.3 SSB, CW
50.10-50.125 DX window
50.125 SSB calling
50.3-50.6 All modes
50.6-50.8 Nonvoice communications
50.62 Digital (packet) calling
50.8-51.0 Radio remote control (20-kHz channels)
51.0-51.1 Pacific DX window
51.12-51.48 Repeater inputs (19 channels)
51.12-51.18 Digital repeater inputs
51.5-51.6 Simplex (seven channels)
51.62-51.98 Repeater outputs (19 channels)
51.62-51.68 Digital repeater outputs
52.0-52.48 Repeater inputs (except as noted; 23 channels)
52.02, 52.04 FM simplex
52.2 TEST PAIR (input)
52.5-52.98 Repeater output (except as noted; 23 channels)
52.525 Primary FM simplex
52.54 Secondary FM simplex
52.7 TEST PAIR (output)
53.0-53.48 Repeater inputs (except as noted; 19 channels)
53.0 Remote base FM simplex
53.02 Simplex
53.1, 53.2, 53.3, 53.4 Radio remote control
53.5-53.98 Repeater outputs (except as noted; 19 channels)
53.5, 53.6, 53.7, 53.8 Radio remote control
53.52, 53.9 Simplex

2 Meters (144-148 MHz)

144.00-144.05 EME (CW)
144.05-144.10 General CW and weak signals
144.10-144.20 EME and weak-signal SSB
144.200 National calling frequency
144.200-144.275 General SSB operation
144.275-144.300 Propagation beacons
144.30-144.50 New OSCAR subband
144.50-144.60 Linear translator inputs
144.60-144.90 FM repeater inputs
144.90-145.10 Weak signal and FM simplex (145.01,03,05,07,09 are widely used for packet)
145.10-145.20 Linear translator outputs
145.20-145.50 FM repeater outputs
145.50-145.80 Miscellaneous and experimental modes
145.80-146.00 OSCAR subband
146.01-146.37 Repeater inputs
146.40-146.58 Simplex
146.52 National Simplex Calling Frequency
146.61-146.97 Repeater outputs
147.00-147.39 Repeater outputs
147.42-147.57 Simplex
147.60-147.99 Repeater inputs

1.25 Meters (222-225 MHz)

222.0-222.150 Weak-signal modes
222.0-222.025 EME
222.05-222.06 Propagation beacons
222.1 SSB & CW calling frequency
222.10-222.15 Weak-signal CW & SSB
222.15-222.25 Local coordinator's option; weak signal, ACSB, repeater inputs, control
222.25-223.38 FM repeater inputs only
223.40-223.52 FM simplex
223.52-223.64 Digital, packet
223.64-223.70 Links, control
223.71-223.85 Local coordinator's option; FM simplex, packet, repeater outputs
223.85-224.98 Repeater outputs only

70 Centimeters (420-450 MHz)

420.00-426.00 ATV repeater or simplex with 421.25 MHz video carrier control links and experimental
426.00-432.00 ATV simplex with 427.250-MHz video carrier frequency
432.00-432.07 EME (Earth-Moon-Earth)
432.07-432.10 Weak-signal CW
432.10 70-cm calling frequency

432.10-432.30 Mixed-mode and weak-signal work
432.30-432.40 Propagation beacons
432.40-433.00 Mixed-mode and weak-signal work
433.00-435.00 Auxiliary/repeater links
435.00-438.00 Satellite only (internationally)
438.00-444.00 ATV repeater input with 439.250-MHz video carrier frequency and repeater links
442.00-445.00 Repeater inputs and outputs (local option)
445.00-447.00 Shared by auxiliary and control links, repeaters and simplex (local option)
446.00 National simplex frequency
447.00-450.00 Repeater inputs and outputs (local option)

33 Centimeters (902-928 MHz)

902.0-903.0 Narrow-bandwidth, weak-signal communications
902.0-902.8 SSTV, FAX, ACSSB, experimental
902.1 Weak-signal calling frequency
902.8-903.0 Reserved for EME, CW expansion
903.1 Alternate calling frequency
903.0-906.0 Digital communications
906-909 FM repeater inputs
909-915 ATV
915-918 Digital communications
918-921 FM repeater outputs
921-927 ATV
927-928 FM simplex and links

23 Centimeters (1240-1300 MHz)

1240-1246 ATV #1
1246-1248 Narrow-bandwidth FM point-to-point links and digital, duplex with 1258-1260.
1248-1258 Digital Communications
1252-1258 ATV #2
1258-1260 Narrow-bandwidth FM point-to-point links digital, duplexed with 1246-1252
1260-1270 Satellite uplinks, reference WARC '79
1260-1270 Wide-bandwidth experimental, simplex ATV
1270-1276 Repeater inputs, FM and linear, paired with 1282-1288, 239 pairs every 25 kHz, e.g. 1270.025, .050, etc.
1271-1283 Non-coordinated test pair
1276-1282 ATV #3
1282-1288 Repeater outputs, paired with 1270-1276
1288-1294 Wide-bandwidth experimental, simplex ATV
1294-1295 Narrow-bandwidth FM simplex services, 25-kHz channels
1294.5 National FM simplex calling frequency
1295-1297 Narrow bandwidth weak-signal communications (no FM)
1295.0-1295.8 SSTV, FAX, ACSSB, experimental
1295.8-1296.0 Reserved for EME, CW expansion

1296.00-1296.05 EME-exclusive
1296.07-1296.08 CW beacons
1296.1 CW, SSB calling frequency
1296.4-1296.6 Crossband linear translator input
1296.6-1296.8 Crossband linear translator output
1296.8-1297.0 Experimental beacons (exclusive)
1297-1300 Digital Communications

2300-2310 and 2390-2450 MHz

2300.0-2303.0 High-rate data
2303.0-2303.5 Packet
2303.5-2303.8 TTY packet
2303.9-2303.9 Packet, TTY, CW, EME
2303.9-2304.1 CW, EME
2304.1 Calling frequency
2304.1-2304.2 CW, EME, SSB
2304.2-2304.3 SSB, SSTV, FAX, Packet AM, Amtor
2304.30-2304.32 Propagation beacon network
2304.32-2304.40 General propagation beacons
2304.4-2304.5 SSB, SSTV, ACSSB, FAX, Packet AM, Amtor experimental
2304.5-2304.7 Crossband linear translator input
2304.7-2304.9 Crossband linear translator output
2304.9-2305.0 Experimental beacons
2305.0-2305.2 FM simplex (25 kHz spacing)
2305.20 FM simplex calling frequency
2305.2-2306.0 FM simplex (25 kHz spacing)
2306.0-2309.0 FM Repeaters (25 kHz) input
2309.0-2310.0 Control and auxiliary links
2390.0-2396.0 Fast-scan TV
2396.0-2399.0 High-rate data
2399.0-2399.5 Packet
2399.5-2400.0 Control and auxiliary links
2400.0-2403.0 Satellite
2403.0-2408.0 Satellite high-rate data
2408.0-2410.0 Satellite
2410.0-2413.0 FM repeaters (25 kHz) output
2413.0-2418.0 High-rate data
2418.0-2430.0 Fast-scan TV
2430.0-2433.0 Satellite
2433.0-2438.0 Satellite high-rate data
2438.0-2450.0 WB FM, FSTV, FMTV, SS experimental

3300-3500 MHz

3456.3-3456.4 Propagation beacons

5650-5925 MHz
5760.3-5760.4 Propagation beacons

10.00-10.50 GHz
10.368 Narrow band calling frequency 10.3683-10.3684 Propagation beacons 10.3640 Calling frequency

Now that you have your license (you do, don't you?), and your equipment, you are ready to go live. Below is a suggested start.

1) Assuming you have the HT set up to the appropriate frequency, and offset, press the mic button on the HT and say, "KK4HWX listening." Replace the KK4HWX with your own call sign, the one assigned to you by the FCC (it's the law). If no one responds to your call, you may wish to try again. Hopefully someone will respond to your call.

2) Once you get a response, it will be in the form of something like, "KK4HWX this is ??1??? in Eastport returning. My name is Florence. Back to you. ??1???" then a tone. Let us examine the response more closely. She first acknowledged your call sign (KK4HWX), then identified hers (??1???). From the 1 in her call sign, you know that she first got her license in Region 1, meaning she got it while a resident of CT, ME, MA, NH, RI, or VT. She then told you where she's transmitting from (Eastport). The term "returning" means that she is returning your call. Her name is Florence. The phrase, "Back to you" indicates that she is turning over the conversation to you. She then repeats her call sign. The tone indicates to you that it is okay to proceed with your response. BTW if she had used the term "Over" instead of "Back to you," it would mean the same thing, just fewer words.

3) At this point, press the mic button and continue with the conversation. You should restate your call sign often during the conversation (perhaps every 10 minutes or less and whenever you begin transmitting). Don't forget to say, "Over" or "Back to you" whenever you are giving Florence control of the conversation again.

4) When you are ready to stop the conversation, you should say goodbye or use the phrase "73", meaning "best wishes." Your conversation would end something like, "??1??? 73, this is KK4HWX clear and monitoring." The "clear and monitoring" indicates that you are going to continue to monitor the frequency. If you are not going to continue monitoring, you may wish to end the conversation with Florence with, "clear and QRT" instead. The QRT means that you are stopping transmissions.

Call Sign Phonics

Because of different accents of various people, sometimes it is difficult to understand call sign letters when spoken. For this reason, most ham operators verbalize their call sign using phonics. Below is a table listing the accepted phonics for letters and numbers.

A = ALFA	S = SIERRA
B = BRAVO	T = TANGO
C = CHARLIE	U = UNIFORM
D = DELTA	V = VICTOR
E = ECHO	W = WHISKEY
F = FOXTROT	X = X-RAY
G = GOLF	Y = YANKEE
H = HOTEL	Z = ZULU (ZED)
I = INDIA	1 = ONE
J = JULIETT	2 = TWO
K = KILO	3 = THREE (TREE)
L = LIMA	4 = FOUR
M = MIKE	5 = FIVE (FIFE)
N = NOVEMBER	6 = SEVEN
O = OSCAR	7 = SEVEN
P = PAPA (PA-PA')	8 = EIGHT
Q = QUEBEC (KAY-BEK')	9 = NINE (NINER)
R = ROMEO	0 = ZERO

The words in parentheses are the pronunciation or the alternate pronunciations for the words or numbers, but you will hear both used. With the letter Z, (ZED) is by far the most commonly used. With the number 9, NINER is the most common and easiest to understand ON THE AIR.

If you wish to use Morse code (CW) instead of voice communication, the "conversation" would follow the same steps, with a few modifications. To type out each word would require a lot of typing and translating. If you are like this author, more means more, i.e., more typing means more typos are likely. To help with this situation, CW enthusiasts have developed a language all their own – they use abbreviations for common phrases. Below is a chart showing some of these abbreviations.

Abbreviation	Use
AR	Over
de	From or "this is"
ES	And
GM	Good Morning
K	Go
KN	Go only
NM	Name
QTH	Location
RPT	Report
R	Roger
SK	Clear
tnx	Thanks
UR	Your, you are
73	Best Wishes

Morse Code and Amateur Radio

If you wish to use CW, but are concerned about accuracy, you might consider purchasing a Morse code translator. This is an electronic device that you place in front of your speakers. It takes the CW sounds and translates them into English and displays the transmission on an LCD display. For the reverse, you can pick up a CW keyboard. With the keyboard, you type in your message and it converts the text to Morse code. The translator does not need to be attached to your ham equipment, whereas the keyboard would.

For your convenience, below is a table showing the Morse code signals and their meaning.

Character	Code
A	· —
B	— · · ·
C	— · — ·
D	— · ·
E	·
F	· · — ·
G	— — ·
H	· · · ·
I	· ·
J	· — — —
K	— · —
L	· — · ·
M	— —
N	— ·
O	— — —
P	· — — ·
Q	— — · —
R	· — ·
S	· · ·
T	—
U	· · —
V	· · · —
W	· — —
X	— · · —
Y	— · — —
Z	— — · ·
0	— — — — —
1	· — — — —
2	· · — — —
3	· · · — —
4	· · · · —
5	· · · · ·

6	— · · · ·
7	— — · · ·
8	— — — · ·
9	— — — — ·
Ampersand [&], Wait	· — · · ·
Apostrophe [']	· — — — — ·
At sign [@]	· — — · — ·
Colon [:]	— — — · · ·
Comma [,]	— — · · — —
Dollar sign [$]	· · · — · · —
Double dash [=]	— · · · —
Exclamation mark [!]	— · — · — —
Hyphen, Minus [-]	— · · · · —
Parenthesis closed [)]	— · — — · —
Parenthesis open [(]	— · — — ·
Period [.]	· — · — · —
Plus [+]	· — · — ·
Question mark [?]	· · — — · ·
Quotation mark ["]	· — · · — ·
Semicolon [;]	— · — · — ·
Slash [/], Fraction bar	— · · — ·
Underscore [_]	· · — — · —

An advantage of using Morse Code is that when broadcasting CW, you are using reduced power, thereby saving your battery. Your battery is used only while actually transmitting or receiving.

International Call Sign Prefixes

As was stated earlier, all ham radio call signs begin with letters (or numbers) taken from blocks assigned to each country of the world by the *ITU - International Telecommunications Union,* a body controlled by the United Nations. The following chart indicates which call sign series are allocated to which countries.

Call Sign Series	Allocated to
AAA-ALZ	**United States of America**
AMA-AOZ	Spain
APA-ASZ	Pakistan (Islamic Republic of)
ATA-AWZ	India (Republic of)
AXA-AXZ	Australia
AYA-AZZ	Argentine Republic
A2A-A2Z	Botswana (Republic of)
A3A-A3Z	Tonga (Kingdom of)
A4A-A4Z	Oman (Sultanate of)
A5A-A5Z	Bhutan (Kingdom of)

A6A-A6Z	United Arab Emirates
A7A-A7Z	Qatar (State of)
A8A-A8Z	Liberia (Republic of)
A9A-A9Z	Bahrain (State of)
BAA-BZZ	China (People's Republic of)
CAA-CEZ	Chile
CFA-CKZ	Canada
CLA-CMZ	Cuba
CNA-CNZ	Morocco (Kingdom of)
COA-COZ	Cuba
CPA-CPZ	Bolivia (Republic of)
CQA-CUZ	Portugal
CVA-CXZ	Uruguay (Eastern Republic of)
CYA-CZZ	Canada
C2A-C2Z	Nauru (Republic of)
C3A-C3Z	Andorra (Principality of)
C4A-C4Z	Cyprus (Republic of)
C5A-C5Z	Gambia (Republic of the)
C6A-C6Z	Bahamas (Commonwealth of the)
C7A-C7Z	World Meteorological Organization
C8A-C9Z	Mozambique (Republic of)
DAA-DRZ	Germany (Federal Republic of)
DSA-DTZ	Korea (Republic of)
DUA-DZZ	Philippines (Republic of the)
D2A-D3Z	Angola (Republic of)
D4A-D4Z	Cape Verde (Republic of)
D5A-D5Z	Liberia (Republic of)
D6A-D6Z	Comoros (Islamic Federal Republic of the)
D7A-D9Z	Korea (Republic of)
EAA-EHZ	Spain
EIA-EJZ	Ireland
EKA-EKZ	Armenia (Republic of)
ELA-ELZ	Liberia (Republic of)
EMA-EOZ	Ukraine
EPA-EQZ	Iran (Islamic Republic of)
ERA-ERZ	Moldova (Republic of)
ESA-ESZ	Estonia (Republic of)
ETA-ETZ	Ethiopia (Federal Democratic Republic of)
EUA-EWZ	Belarus (Republic of)
EXA-EXZ	Kyrgyz Republic
EYA-EYZ	Tajikistan (Republic of)
EZA-EZZ	Turkmenistan
E2A-E2Z	Thailand
E3A-E3Z	Eritrea
E4A-E4Z	Palestinian Authority

E5A-E5Z	New Zealand - Cook Islands (WRC-07)
E7A-E7Z	Bosnia and Herzegovina (Republic of) (WRC-07)
FAA-FZZ	France
GAA-GZZ	United Kingdom of Great Britain and Northern Ireland
HAA-HAZ	Hungary (Republic of)
HBA-HBZ	Switzerland (Confederation of)
HCA-HDZ	Ecuador
HEA-HEZ	Switzerland (Confederation of)
HFA-HFZ	Poland (Republic of)
HGA-HGZ	Hungary (Republic of)
HHA-HHZ	Haiti (Republic of)
HIA-HIZ	Dominican Republic
HJA-HKZ	Colombia (Republic of)
HLA-HLZ	Korea (Republic of)
HMA-HMZ	Democratic People's Republic of Korea
HNA-HNZ	Iraq (Republic of)
HOA-HPZ	Panama (Republic of)
HQA-HRZ	Honduras (Republic of)
HSA-HSZ	Thailand
HTA-HTZ	Nicaragua
HUA-HUZ	El Salvador (Republic of)
HVA-HVZ	Vatican City State
HWA-HYZ	France
HZA-HZZ	Saudi Arabia (Kingdom of)
H2A-H2Z	Cyprus (Republic of)
H3A-H3Z	Panama (Republic of)
H4A-H4Z	Solomon Islands
H6A-H7Z	Nicaragua
H8A-H9Z	Panama (Republic of)
IAA-IZZ	Italy
JAA-JSZ	Japan
JTA-JVZ	Mongolia
JWA-JXZ	Norway
JYA-JYZ	Jordan (Hashemite Kingdom of)
JZA-JZZ	Indonesia (Republic of)
J2A-J2Z	Djibouti (Republic of)
J3A-J3Z	Grenada
J4A-J4Z	Greece
J5A-J5Z	Guinea-Bissau (Republic of)
J6A-J6Z	Saint Lucia
J7A-J7Z	Dominica (Commonwealth of)
J8A-J8Z	Saint Vincent and the Grenadines
KAA-KZZ	**United States of America**
LAA-LNZ	Norway
LOA-LWZ	Argentine Republic

LXA-LXZ	Luxembourg
LYA-LYZ	Lithuania (Republic of)
LZA-LZZ	Bulgaria (Republic of)
L2A-L9Z	Argentine Republic
MAA-MZZ	United Kingdom of Great Britain and Northern Ireland
NAA-NZZ	**United States of America**
OAA-OCZ	Peru
ODA-ODZ	Lebanon
OEA-OEZ	Austria
OFA-OJZ	Finland
OKA-OLZ	Czech Republic
OMA-OMZ	Slovak Republic
ONA-OTZ	Belgium
OUA-OZZ	Denmark
PAA-PIZ	Netherlands (Kingdom of the)
PJA-PJZ	Netherlands (Kingdom of the) - Netherlands Antilles
PKA-POZ	Indonesia (Republic of)
PPA-PYZ	Brazil (Federative Republic of)
PZA-PZZ	Suriname (Republic of)
P2A-P2Z	Papua New Guinea
P3A-P3Z	Cyprus (Republic of)
P4A-P4Z	Netherlands (Kingdom of the) - Aruba
P5A-P9Z	Democratic People's Republic of Korea
RAA-RZZ	Russian Federation
SAA-SMZ	Sweden
SNA-SRZ	Poland (Republic of)
SSA-SSM	Egypt (Arab Republic of)
SSN-STZ	Sudan (Republic of the)
SUA-SUZ	Egypt (Arab Republic of)
SVA-SZZ	Greece
S2A-S3Z	Bangladesh (People's Republic of)
S5A-S5Z	Slovenia (Republic of)
S6A-S6Z	Singapore (Republic of)
S7A-S7Z	Seychelles (Republic of)
S8A-S8Z	South Africa (Republic of)
S9A-S9Z	Sao Tome and Principe (Democratic Republic of)
TAA-TCZ	Turkey
TDA-TDZ	Guatemala (Republic of)
TEA-TEZ	Costa Rica
TFA-TFZ	Iceland
TGA-TGZ	Guatemala (Republic of)
THA-THZ	France
TIA-TIZ	Costa Rica
TJA-TJZ	Cameroon (Republic of)
TKA-TKZ	France

TLA-TLZ	Central African Republic
TMA-TMZ	France
TNA-TNZ	Congo (Republic of the)
TOA-TQZ	France
TRA-TRZ	Gabonese Republic
TSA-TSZ	Tunisia
TTA-TTZ	Chad (Republic of)
TUA-TUZ	Côte d'Ivoire (Republic of)
TVA-TXZ	France
TYA-TYZ	Benin (Republic of)
TZA-TZZ	Mali (Republic of)
T2A-T2Z	Tuvalu
T3A-T3Z	Kiribati (Republic of)
T4A-T4Z	Cuba
T5A-T5Z	Somali Democratic Republic
T6A-T6Z	Afghanistan (Islamic State of)
T7A-T7Z	San Marino (Republic of)
T8A-T8Z	Palau (Republic of)
UAA-UIZ	Russian Federation
UJA-UMZ	Uzbekistan (Republic of)
UNA-UQZ	Kazakhstan (Republic of)
URA-UZZ	Ukraine
VAA-VGZ	Canada
VHA-VNZ	Australia
VOA-VOZ	Canada
VPA-VQZ	United Kingdom of Great Britain and Northern Ireland
VRA-VRZ	China (People's Republic of) - Hong Kong
VSA-VSZ	United Kingdom of Great Britain and Northern Ireland
VTA-VWZ	India (Republic of)
VXA-VYZ	Canada
VZA-VZZ	Australia
V2A-V2Z	Antigua and Barbuda
V3A-V3Z	Belize
V4A-V4Z	Saint Kitts and Nevis
V5A-V5Z	Namibia (Republic of)
V6A-V6Z	Micronesia (Federated States of)
V7A-V7Z	Marshall Islands (Republic of the)
V8A-V8Z	Brunei Darussalam
WAA-WZZ	**United States of America**
XAA-XIZ	Mexico
XJA-XOZ	Canada
XPA-XPZ	Denmark
XQA-XRZ	Chile
XSA-XSZ	China (People's Republic of)
XTA-XTZ	Burkina Faso

XUA-XUZ	Cambodia (Kingdom of)
XVA-XVZ	Viet Nam (Socialist Republic of)
XWA-XWZ	Lao People's Democratic Republic
XXA-XXZ	China (People's Republic of) - Macao (WRC-07)
XYA-XZZ	Myanmar (Union of)
YAA-YAZ	Afghanistan (Islamic State of)
YBA-YHZ	Indonesia (Republic of)
YIA-YIZ	Iraq (Republic of)
YJA-YJZ	Vanuatu (Republic of)
YKA-YKZ	Syrian Arab Republic
YLA-YLZ	Latvia (Republic of)
YMA-YMZ	Turkey
YNA-YNZ	Nicaragua
YOA-YRZ	Romania
YSA-YSZ	El Salvador (Republic of)
YTA-YUZ	Serbia (Republic of) (WRC-07)
YVA-YYZ	Venezuela (Republic of)
Y2A-Y9Z	Germany (Federal Republic of)
ZAA-ZAZ	Albania (Republic of)
ZBA-ZJZ	United Kingdom of Great Britain and Northern Ireland
ZKA-ZMZ	New Zealand
ZNA-ZOZ	United Kingdom of Great Britain and Northern Ireland
ZPA-ZPZ	Paraguay (Republic of)
ZQA-ZQZ	United Kingdom of Great Britain and Northern Ireland
ZRA-ZUZ	South Africa (Republic of)
ZVA-ZZZ	Brazil (Federative Republic of)
Z2A-Z2Z	Zimbabwe (Republic of)
Z3A-Z3Z	The Former Yugoslav Republic of Macedonia
2AA-2ZZ	United Kingdom of Great Britain and Northern Ireland
3AA-3AZ	Monaco (Principality of)
3BA-3BZ	Mauritius (Republic of)
3CA-3CZ	Equatorial Guinea (Republic of)
3DA-3DM	Swaziland (Kingdom of)
3DN-3DZ	Fiji (Republic of)
3EA-3FZ	Panama (Republic of)
3GA-3GZ	Chile
3HA-3UZ	China (People's Republic of)
3VA-3VZ	Tunisia
3WA-3WZ	Viet Nam (Socialist Republic of)
3XA-3XZ	Guinea (Republic of)
3YA-3YZ	Norway
3ZA-3ZZ	Poland (Republic of)
4AA-4CZ	Mexico
4DA-4IZ	Philippines (Republic of the)
4JA-4KZ	Azerbaijani Republic

4LA-4LZ	Georgia (Republic of)
4MA-4MZ	Venezuela (Republic of)
4OA-4OZ	Montenegro (Republic of) (WRC-07)
4PA-4SZ	Sri Lanka (Democratic Socialist Republic of)
4TA-4TZ	Peru
4UA-4UZ	United Nations
4VA-4VZ	Haiti (Republic of)
4WA-4WZ	Democratic Republic of Timor-Leste (WRC-03)
4XA-4XZ	Israel (State of)
4YA-4YZ	International Civil Aviation Organization
4ZA-4ZZ	Israel (State of)
5AA-5AZ	Libya (Socialist People's Libyan Arab Jamahiriya)
5BA-5BZ	Cyprus (Republic of)
5CA-5GZ	Morocco (Kingdom of)
5HA-5IZ	Tanzania (United Republic of)
5JA-5KZ	Colombia (Republic of)
5LA-5MZ	Liberia (Republic of)
5NA-5OZ	Nigeria (Federal Republic of)
5PA-5QZ	Denmark
5RA-5SZ	Madagascar (Republic of)
5TA-5TZ	Mauritania (Islamic Republic of)
5UA-5UZ	Niger (Republic of the)
5VA-5VZ	Togolese Republic
5WA-5WZ	Samoa (Independent State of)
5XA-5XZ	Uganda (Republic of)
5YA-5ZZ	Kenya (Republic of)
6AA-6BZ	Egypt (Arab Republic of)
6CA-6CZ	Syrian Arab Republic
6DA-6JZ	Mexico
6KA-6NZ	Korea (Republic of)
6OA-6OZ	Somali Democratic Republic
6PA-6SZ	Pakistan (Islamic Republic of)
6TA-6UZ	Sudan (Republic of the)
6VA-6WZ	Senegal (Republic of)
6XA-6XZ	Madagascar (Republic of)
6YA-6YZ	Jamaica
6ZA-6ZZ	Liberia (Republic of)
7AA-7IZ	Indonesia (Republic of)
7JA-7NZ	Japan
7OA-7OZ	Yemen (Republic of)
7PA-7PZ	Lesotho (Kingdom of)
7QA-7QZ	Malawi
7RA-7RZ	Algeria (People's Democratic Republic of)
7SA-7SZ	Sweden
7TA-7YZ	Algeria (People's Democratic Republic of)

7ZA-7ZZ	Saudi Arabia (Kingdom of)
8AA-8IZ	Indonesia (Republic of)
8JA-8NZ	Japan
8OA-8OZ	Botswana (Republic of)
8PA-8PZ	Barbados
8QA-8QZ	Maldives (Republic of)
8RA-8RZ	Guyana
8SA-8SZ	Sweden
8TA-8YZ	India (Republic of)
8ZA-8ZZ	Saudi Arabia (Kingdom of)
9AA-9AZ	Croatia (Republic of)
9BA-9DZ	Iran (Islamic Republic of)
9EA-9FZ	Ethiopia (Federal Democratic Republic of)
9GA-9GZ	Ghana
9HA-9HZ	Malta
9IA-9JZ	Zambia (Republic of)
9KA-9KZ	Kuwait (State of)
9LA-9LZ	Sierra Leone
9MA-9MZ	Malaysia
9NA-9NZ	Nepal
9OA-9TZ	Democratic Republic of the Congo
9UA-9UZ	Burundi (Republic of)
9VA-9VZ	Singapore (Republic of)
9WA-9WZ	Malaysia
9XA-9XZ	Rwandese Republic
9YA-9ZZ	Trinidad and Tobago

Third-Party Communications and Amateur Radio

If all of this information about ham radios is somewhat intimidating, do not despair. "You" can still use ham radios for communications without being a licensed operator. Yes, you do have to have a ham license in order to legally transmit by ham equipment (or be under the direct supervision of someone else who is licensed), but there is an alternative – third-party communication.

Third-party communications occur when a licensed operator sends either written or verbal messages on behalf of unlicensed persons or organizations. There are two "controls" on third-party communication.

First, the communication must be noncommercial and of a personal nature. Asking a ham operator to contact another ham operator located in an area just hit by tornados and, because of being without power, phones do not work in Grandma Sally's city so you can check up on her, is okay. Asking a ham to send a message out that you have an old Chevy for sale would not be okay.

Second, the message must be going to a permitted area. Transmitting from a US location to another US location is okay, but transmitting from the US to another country may not. Because third-party communications bypass a country's normal telephone and postal systems, many foreign governments forbid such communications. In order to transmit from one country to another, the other country must have signed a third-party agreement with the US. What follows is a list of those countries that do have third-party a communications agreement with the US.

V2	Antigua / Barbuda
LU	Argentina
VK	Australia
V3	Belize
CP	Bolivia
T9	Bosnia-Herzegovina
PY	Brazil
VE	Canada
CE	Chile
HK	Colombia
D6	Comoros (Federal Islamic Republic of)
TI	Costa Rica
CO	Cuba
HI	Dominican Republic
J7	Dominica
HC	Ecuador
YS	El Salvador
C5	Gambia, The
9G	Ghana
J3	Grenada
TG	Guatemala
8R	Guyana
HH	Haiti
HR	Honduras
4X	Israel
6Y	Jamaica
JY	Jordan
EL	Liberia
V7	Marshall Islands
XE	Mexico
V6	Micronesia, Federated States of
YN	Nicaragua
HP	Panama
ZP	Paraguay
OA	Peru
DU	Philippines
VR6	Pitcairn Island

V4	St. Christopher / Nevis
J6	St. Lucia
J8	St. Vincent and the Grenadines
9L	Sierra Leone
ZS	South Africa
3DA	Swaziland
9Y	Trinidad / Tobago
TA	Turkey
GB	United Kingdom
CX	Uruguay
YV	Venezuela
4U1ITUITU	Geneva
4U1VICVIC	Vienna

Remember, before TSHTF, keep your pantry well stocked, your powder dry, and your batteries fully charged. 73

APPENDIX A

American Radio Relay League

Affiliated Amateur Radio Clubs in

Delaware

ARRL Affiliated Club	**Delaware Weak Signal Group**
City:	Claymont, DE
Section:	DE

ARRL Affiliated Club	**Kent County Amateur Radio Club**
City:	Dover, DE
Call Sign:	W3HZW
Section:	DE
Links:	www.kcarc.net

ARRL Affiliated Club	**Sussex Technical Amateur Radio Club**
City:	Georgetown, DE
Call Sign:	K3STR
Section:	DE
Links:	www.k3str.com

ARRL Affiliated Club	**Lewes Amateur Radio Society**
City:	Lewes, DE
Call Sign:	W3LRS
Section:	DE
Links:	www.lewesars.com

ARRL Affiliated Club	**96 Over The Hill Gang/Metro**
City:	New Castle, DE
Call Sign:	W3PS
Section:	DE
Links:	W3Publicservice@yahoogroups.com,

ARRL Affiliated Club	**University of Delaware Amateur Radio Club**
City:	Newark, DE
Call Sign:	W3UD
Section:	DE
Links:	www.eecis.udel.edu/~w3ud/

ARRL Affiliated Club	**First State Amateur Radio Club**
City:	Newark, DE
Call Sign:	K3QBD
Section:	DE
Links:	www.fsarc.org

ARRL Affiliated Club	**Delaware Repeater Association, Inc.**
City:	Newport, DE
Call Sign:	W3DRA
Section:	DE
Links:	www.dra73.org

ARRL Affiliated Club   **Nanticoke Amateur Radio Club, Inc.**
City: Seaford, DE
Call Sign: W3TBG
Section: DE
Links: www.qsl.net/w3tbg/

ARRL Affiliated Club   **Sussex Amateur Radio Association**
City: Selbyville, DE
Call Sign: KB3BHL
Section: DE
Links: sussexamateurradio.com

ARRL Affiliated Club   **DelMarVA DX Association**
City: Selbyville, DE
Call Sign: W3PP
Section: DE

ARRL Affiliated Club   **New Castle County Emergency Operations G**
City: Wilmington, DE
Call Sign: WN3EOC
Section: DE
Links: ncceog.org

APPENDIX B

Amateur Radio License Holders

in

Delaware
(by City)

FCC Amateur Radio License in Arden

Call Sign: N3CUD
Roberta Perkins
2107 Harvey Rd
Arden DE 198104011

FCC Amateur Radio License in Bear

Call Sign: KI3B
Joseph M Grib Jr
42 Anderson Ct
Bear DE 19701

Call Sign: W3SL
Delaware Amateur Radio
Club
42 Anderson Ct
Bear DE 19701

Call Sign: AE3X
Thomas R Amatuzio Sr
4 Anna Ave
Bear DE 19701

Call Sign: KC3GN
Anthony J Sheridan
26 Anna Ave Caravel
Farms
Bear DE 197011776

Call Sign: KB3UZI
Aaron S Knipe
224 Channing Dr
Bear DE 19701

Call Sign: KB3JAQ
Susan A Perry
4305 Christiana Meadows
Bear DE 19701

Call Sign: N3CAK
Francis J Clarkin Sr

4608 Christiana Meadows
Bear DE 19701

Call Sign: N3JLH
Donald R Hanby Jr
108 Christy Ct
Bear DE 19701

Call Sign: KB2EPI
Carlos Fernandez
640 Clifton Dr
Bear DE 19701

Call Sign: KB3BS
John B Krick
35 Clipper Ct
Bear DE 19701

Call Sign: KB3IUO
Gloria D Zehnacker
44 Clipper Ct
Bear DE 197011686

Call Sign: KB3FUB
Russell Zehnacker
44 Clipper Ct
Bear DE 197011686

Call Sign: KB3NKJ
Thomas M Robinson
923 Clydesdale Dr
Bear DE 19701

Call Sign: N8BWQ
Gary J Heil
165 Countryside Ln
Bear DE 197012011

Call Sign: K2DLD
Brian M Hornbeck
25 Craig Rd
Bear DE 19701

Call Sign: N3RPD
James F Griffiths

26 Crimson King Dr
Bear DE 197012387

Call Sign: WB3AES
Donald S Zabitka
12 Debra Dr
Bear DE 19701

Call Sign: N3LOA
Norris G Winebrenner
15 Debra Dr
Bear DE 19701

Call Sign: N3WFZ
Michael S Ruderman
9 Decidedly Ln
Bear DE 19701

Call Sign: N3OGG
Michael E Kump
2593 Denny Rd
Bear DE 19701

Call Sign: N9RZ
Russell Zehnacker
1102 Donna Marie Loop
Bear DE 19701

Call Sign: W9GDZ
Gloria D Zehnacker
1102 Donna Marie Loop
Bear DE 19701

Call Sign: KB3KAJ
Maple Valley Trotting
Association
720 Elizabeth Ln
Bear DE 19701

Call Sign: WC3T
Maple Valley Trotting
Association
720 Elizabeth Ln
Bear DE 19701

Call Sign: WX3NCC
David T Garland
2 Fife Ln
Bear DE 19701

Call Sign: KB3UAW
Kenneth G Kirk
26 Fox Hunt Dr 207
Bear DE 197012534

Call Sign: N2VRQ
David A Larson
901 Governors Pl 187
Bear DE 19701

Call Sign: KB3GAK
William A Pepper
615 Green Spring Dr
Bear DE 19701

Call Sign: KB3MMS
David R Pepper
615 Green Spring Dr
Bear DE 19701

Call Sign: WB3IFK
John R Carlton
617 Green Spring Dr
Bear DE 19701

Call Sign: N3VPL
James E Passwaters Jr
117 Hannum Dr
Bear DE 19701

Call Sign: KE3WH
Daniel E Hart Sr
6 Harpers Pl
Bear DE 197011207

Call Sign: KB3PMV
Briant M Shepherd Jr
207 Hope Ct E
Bear DE 197013365

Call Sign: KB3RET
Linda M Mccall
461 Howell School Rd
Bear DE 19701

Call Sign: KB3QVD
Beverly A Benton
606 Hucklebery Dr
Bear DE 19701

Call Sign: KB3IMJ
Richard A Sacco
4 Jannsen Ct
Bear DE 19701

Call Sign: AB3IY
Richard A Sacco
4 Jannsen Ct
Bear DE 19701

Call Sign: W2YCI
Bernard Elowitz
41 Jester St
Bear DE 19701

Call Sign: WA3WUR
Joseph H Newman Jr
14 Kerry Ct
Bear DE 197016346

Call Sign: KA3RFL
Michael D Prime
101 Lewis Ct
Bear DE 19701

Call Sign: KB2FDR
John W Lierenz Jr
10 Lotus Cir N
Bear DE 19701

Call Sign: N3OFN
Mark S Barnett
22 Lotus Cir N
Bear DE 197016320

Call Sign: KB3PKG
Leon B Reed II
56 Mahopac Dr
Bear DE 19701

Call Sign: KB3PTR
Gerald H Tatum
102 Mandalay Dr
Bear DE 19701

Call Sign: KB3LJO
Grant C Harrington
110 Maplecroft Ln
Bear DE 19701

Call Sign: K4CAP
Gilbert A Fishbeck
712 N Huckleberry Ave
Bear DE 19701

Call Sign: N3EVQ
Preston H Le Sage
62 N Jacqueline Ct
Bear DE 19701

Call Sign: KB3NKG
Michael J Moyes
23 N Kings Croft Dr
Bear DE 19701

Call Sign: N3RNC
Thomas B Cooper IV
10 Pamela Pl
Bear DE 19701

Call Sign: WB3GOH
Richard E Bowman
38 Pegasus Pl
Bear DE 197012377

Call Sign: N3DBW
Thomas M Tritelli
20 Peninsula Ct
Bear DE 19701

Call Sign: N3MEN
Albert W Drake
1655 Porter Rd
Bear DE 19701

Call Sign: K3URP
Gertrude E Nichols
2496 Porter Rd
Bear DE 19701

Call Sign: N3QHG
Robert W Mc Cabe Jr
14 Ritchie Dr
Bear DE 19701

Call Sign: W3ZOO
Donald R Ayers
103 Roeper St
Bear DE 19701

Call Sign: WD4BAE
James J Cecchini Jr
456 S Hyde Pl
Bear DE 19701

Call Sign: N3XZH
Michael J Szotkiewicz
852 Sabina Cir
Bear DE 19701

Call Sign: N3VRY
John W Rowe
806 Samantha Cir
Bear DE 19701

Call Sign: N3XCU
Adrianna Russo
806 Samantha Cir
Bear DE 19701

Call Sign: N3YDN
Edward P Aragon
1002 San Remo Ct
Bear DE 19701

Call Sign: W3TYI
Johnnie W Reisor
101 Savannah Dr
Bear DE 19701

Call Sign: WA3BZT
Edward J White
809 Seymour Rd
Bear DE 197011121

Call Sign: KA3PDP
Vincent T Morrow
252 Shai Cir
Bear DE 19701

Call Sign: KB3LK
Robert F Holst
216 Silver Birch Ln
Bear DE 0

Call Sign: K3RFH
Robert F Holst
216 Silver Birch Ln
Bear DE 197012384

Call Sign: KA3CBC
Ernest L Rager
319 Skeet Ave Fox Run
Bear DE 19701

Call Sign: KB3MEH
Hans B Hagervik
47 St Georges Terr
Bear DE 19701

Call Sign: N3PCN
Joseph F Lanyon
12 Summerthur Dr
Bear DE 19701

Call Sign: KB3PMU
George E Barnett
2002 Tami Dr
Bear DE 19701

Call Sign: KA3QBG
Troy D Fitzgerald
16 Treelane Dr
Bear DE 19701

Call Sign: KB3IUN
Joseph B Schauber
820 Trophy Way
Bear DE 19701

Call Sign: KA3NAU
Jason C Ipock
213 Varsity Ln
Bear DE 19701

Call Sign: KC4SXN
Joel E Denny
515 Varsity Ln
Bear DE 19701

Call Sign: KA1HN
Thomas B Jensen
100 Veronica Ln
Bear DE 19701

Call Sign: KN2Q
William F Michne
108 Veronica Ln
Bear DE 19701

Call Sign: WB5TZS
William E Bazzelle Sr
17 Waterton Dr
Bear DE 19701

Call Sign: WW3G
Tony Fanning
160 Williomette Dr
Bear DE 19701

Call Sign: W3PHD
Robert Gevjan
111 Woodchuck Pl
Bear DE 19701

Call Sign: KB3GHR
James W Maucher Jr
850 Woods Rd
Bear DE 19701

Call Sign: N8TZF
Madhu Annapragada
4 Wortham Ct
Bear DE 19701

Call Sign: KA3WDH
Mitchell S Paul
115 Wortham Ln
Bear DE 19701

Call Sign: KB3VLT
Timothy A Douglas
3 Yorkshire Ct
Bear DE 19701

Call Sign: W3CER
Christiana Amateur Radio
Emer Serv
Bear DE 19701

Call Sign: KB3STC
Christiana Amateur Radio
Emergency Services
Bear DE 19701

Call Sign: KB3STD
Christiana Amateur Radio
Emergency Services
Bear DE 19701

Call Sign: W3MCU
Christiana Amateur Radio
Emergency Services
Bear DE 19701

Call Sign: W3WLM
Christiana Amateur Radio
Emergency Services
Bear DE 19701

Call Sign: N3IUJ
Wayne B Smith
Bear DE 197010158

Call Sign: KB3SRH
Donna M Smith
Bear DE 19701

Call Sign: KB3SFW
James W Brown
Bear DE 19701

FCC Amateur Radio License in Bethany Beach

Call Sign: KB3TKS
Bethany Beach Amateur
Radio Association
118 Ashwood St
Bethany Beach DE 19930

Call Sign: KF3BB
Bethany Beach Amateur
Radio Association
118 Ashwood St
Bethany Beach DE 19930

Call Sign: N3ME
Tony Mc Clenny
118 Ashwood St
Bethany Beach DE 19930

Call Sign: KB3NEB
Alfred Fallavollita Jr
56118 Cypress Lake Cir
Bethany Beach DE 19930

Call Sign: KB3FZM
Michael P Darcy
691 Garfield Parkway
Bethany Beach DE 19930

Call Sign: N3AME
Donald P Stein
30965 Heather Ln

Bethany Beach DE
199300576

Call Sign: N3HRB
William H Ulmer Sr
218 Oyster Shell Cove Salt
Pond
Bethany Beach DE 19930

Call Sign: KA3FVT
June Thompson
319 Walkabout Rd
Bethany Beach DE 19930

Call Sign: N3UVF
Matthew D Mclaughlin
Bethany Beach DE 19930

Call Sign: KB3HSR
Mark J Taggart
Bethany Beach DE
199301061

Call Sign: KB3OHW
Anthony Pirczhalski Jr
Bethany Beach DE 19930

Call Sign: W3ANT
Anthony Pirczhalski Jr
Bethany Beach DE
199301164

Call Sign: KB3TAW
Stephen R Lett
Bethany Beach DE
199300080

FCC Amateur Radio License in Bethel

Call Sign: K3DEL
Delaware Vhf Society
Bethel DE 199310073

Call Sign: KA3NPY

Rodney S Allen
Bethel DE 199310073

Call Sign: W3CCO
Ronald H Allen II
Bethel DE 199310073

Call Sign: W3OR
Ronald H Allen
Bethel DE 199310073

FCC Amateur Radio License in Blades

Call Sign: N3MZH
Janet L Massey
15 E 3rd St
Blades DE 19973

Call Sign: K1JVU
William R Hooper
104 E 4th St
Blades DE 19973

Call Sign: KB3HTF
Katherine K Kelley
13 E High St
Blades DE 199734140

FCC Amateur Radio License in Bridgeville

Call Sign: KB3QFG
Paul Osborne
11247 6th St
Bridgeville DE 19933

Call Sign: W3EFA
Rubin Naimark
44 Amanda's Teal Dr
Bridgeville DE 19933

Call Sign: W1JDY
Anders A Pedersen
7369 Cannon Rd

Bridgeville DE 19933

Call Sign: WA3KGV
George L Steinmetz
407 Cedar St
Bridgeville DE 19933

Call Sign: N3UBB
Elizabeth C Caruso
14277 Deer Forest Rd
Bridgeville DE 199334224

Call Sign: N3OEG
Bernard G Caruso
14277 Deerforest Rd
Bridgeville DE 199334224

Call Sign: KB3FEE
Adam J Zaimes
407 Delaware Ave Apt B
Bridgeville DE 19933

Call Sign: KB3SGC
Samantha George
2659 Dublin Hill Rd
Bridgeville DE 19933

Call Sign: KB3TXY
Steven M Hopkins
6957 Federalsburg Rd
Bridgeville DE 19933

Call Sign: KB3NRH
Skylar Willey
14375 Haven Rd
Bridgeville DE 19933

Call Sign: KB3UVD
Michael D Vasquez
5147 Hortzell Rd
Bridgeville DE 19933

Call Sign: W2DBB
James V Pulone Jr
2343 McDowell Rd

Bridgeville DE 199333247

Call Sign: N3HNW
Gary L Quillen
95 Meadow Dr
Bridgeville DE 19933

Call Sign: N3RNH
Geneva N Quillen
17388 Meadow Dr
Bridgeville DE 19933

Call Sign: KB3CGJ
Nicholas Mitchell
17780 Meadow Dr
Bridgeville DE 19933

Call Sign: K1UC
Jay L Rutherford
17132 Oak Rd
Bridgeville DE 19933

Call Sign: K3BH
Jay L Rutherford
17132 Oak Rd
Bridgeville DE 19933

Call Sign: N3VEZ
William T Perry Sr
6351 Ray Rd
Bridgeville DE 19933

Call Sign: WA3HTM
Leland F Milspaw
Rd 2
Bridgeville DE 19933

Call Sign: KB3NRG
Jon L Spanish
14470 Russell Rd
Bridgeville DE 19933

Call Sign: KB3NRK
Cassie Stuper
14537 Russell Rd

Bridgeville DE 19933

Call Sign: KB3PIX
Steven P Heder
309 S Main St
Bridgeville DE 19933

Call Sign: KB3OLE
Travis N Milan
4249 Seashore Hwy
Bridgeville DE 19933

Call Sign: KB3NRD
Ralph Myer
5035 Seashore Hwy
Bridgeville DE 19933

Call Sign: W3DA
T Levy
Bridgeville DE 19933

Call Sign: KB3JUU
Janice A Henderson
Bridgeville DE 19933

FCC Amateur Radio License in Camden

Call Sign: K3VWE
Roger B Whitney
225 Cambridge Rd
Camden DE 19934

Call Sign: WB3CYZ
Marlene E Wilson
22 Capt Davis Dr
Camden DE 19934

Call Sign: N3RFU
Mark K Trego
109 Meeting House Ln
Camden DE 19934

Call Sign: WQ2D
Richard E Maly

20 Raze Ln
Camden DE 199340366

Call Sign: W3REM
Richard E Maly
20 Raze Ln
Camden DE 199340366

Call Sign: KB3GFD
Arthur W Downs
4 Ringed Neck Ln
Camden DE 19934

Call Sign: W3LC
Paul L George
615 S Wynn Wood Cir
Camden DE 19934

Call Sign: N4UGF
Charles E Grant
35 Stayton Ln
Camden DE 19934

Call Sign: K2KIQ
Paul L George
36 W Payne Ln
Camden DE 19934

Call Sign: KB3KB
Charles F Jones
4 Wesley St
Camden DE 19934

Call Sign: KB3RIX
Nathan A Badell
318 William St
Camden DE 19934

Call Sign: N3JCP
Richard A Lomax
476 Wynn Wood Cir
Camden DE 19934

Call Sign: N3PTC
James H Tazelaar

Camden DE 19934

Call Sign: W8TAZ
James H Tazelaar
Camden DE 19934

Call Sign: KB3KUC
Jon K Judd
Camden DE 19934

Call Sign: WA3IIX
Jon K Judd
Camden DE 19934

FCC Amateur Radio License in Camden Wyoming

Call Sign: K3NMB
Thomas S Dutton Jr
111 Cedar Ln
Camden Wyoming DE 199341306

Call Sign: KA1KAB
Laurent R Mc Donald
150 Center St
Camden Wyoming DE 19934

Call Sign: KB3QCO
James F Dunn
162 Downey Oak Cir
Camden Wyoming DE 19934

Call Sign: W3JFD
James F Dunn
162 Downey Oak Cir
Camden Wyoming DE 19934

Call Sign: KB3VSU
Eric S Barker
1858 Mahan Corner Rd

Camden Wyoming DE
19934

Call Sign: WA3LPX
William P Ridenour
102 Quail Run
Camden Wyoming DE
19934

Call Sign: N3KPT
Rodney K Godfrey
1423 Tower Rd
Camden Wyoming DE
19934

Call Sign: KB3VLO
Donald D Cridlebaugh III
1793 Tower Rd
Camden Wyoming DE
19934

Call Sign: KB3WLK
Jennifer N Cridlebaugh
1793 Tower Rd
Camden Wyoming DE
19934

FCC Amateur Radio License in Cape Windsor

Call Sign: W3HF
William F Klugh
52 Grant Ave
Cape Windsor DE 19975

FCC Amateur Radio License in Cheswold

Call Sign: AJ3JR
Allen S Jester Jr
321 Main St
Cheswold DE 19936

Call Sign: KE2YG
Barry A Jones

Cheswold DE 19936

FCC Amateur Radio License in Christiana

Call Sign: N3UQV
Charles J Hales
22 N Old Baltimore Pike
Christiana DE 19702

FCC Amateur Radio License in Claymont

Call Sign: KA3SYK
Thomas R Baker
96 Bayard Dr
Claymont DE 19703

Call Sign: WA3TAG
H William Mervine
10 Burns Rd
Claymont DE 19703

Call Sign: WZ3K
Frank R Bressner
807 Causez Ave
Claymont DE 19703

Call Sign: KA3YFO
Shawn E Gaspero
413 Claymont Gardens
Apt E2
Claymont DE 19703

Call Sign: KA3WOT
Effa J Hassel
121 Delaware Ave
Claymont DE 19703

Call Sign: N3QBB
Donald J Cole
11 Everett Ave
Claymont DE 19703

Call Sign: WB3GVD

Joseph A Blithe
2 Franklin Ave
Claymont DE 19703

Call Sign: WA3MGR
Joseph D Elman
201 Garrett Rd
Claymont DE 19703

Call Sign: W3MGR
Joseph D Elman
201 Garrett Rd
Claymont DE 19703

Call Sign: N3FHJ
James J Brady III
123 Glenrock Dr
Claymont DE 19703

Call Sign: KB3AXQ
Janine V Johnson
316 Gov Printz Blvd
Claymont DE 19703

Call Sign: W3TP
Donald W Conrad
7807 Gov Printz Blvd Apt
309
Claymont DE 19703

Call Sign: N3UQX
James E Brower
45 Green St
Claymont DE 19703

Call Sign: N3VAY
Michael A Sweeney
72 Green St
Claymont DE 19703

Call Sign: N3CTP
Janes B Ward
2715 Green St
Claymont DE 19703

Call Sign: KB2PNO
Candice A Harlan
Harbor Dr
Claymont DE 19703

Call Sign: KA3WCV
Jeffrey K Ericson
2516 Hughes Ave
Claymont DE 19703

Call Sign: KA3WPM
Lara C Parks
20 Lawson Ave
Claymont DE 19703

Call Sign: WA3ZTR
David A Clouse
20 Lawson Ave
Claymont DE 19703

Call Sign: KA3PKU
Jacqualine A Schultz
403 Maple Ln
Claymont DE 19703

Call Sign: KB3LIJ
Stephen D Skopowski
836 Marvel Ave
Claymont DE 19703

Call Sign: KA3JRG
Kathleen A Nemeth
42 Miles Rd
Claymont DE 197031217

Call Sign: WB3IKP
David A Nemeth
42 Miles Rd
Claymont DE 197031217

Call Sign: KB3VYH
Richard-Zachary P
Gebelein
43 Miles Rd
Claymont DE 19703

Call Sign: W3LQE
George E Rambo
17 N Avon Dr
Claymont DE 197031501

Call Sign: N3CQG
Paul J Weaver Sr
76 N Avon Dr
Claymont DE 19703

Call Sign: KB3YHJ
Andrew Demetratos
740 Naamans Rd
Claymont DE 19703

Call Sign: KA3KGC
Kenneth D Curtis Sr
841 Parkside Blvd
Claymont DE 19703

Call Sign: N3UCI
Louis J Dombroski
209 Pennsylvania Ave
Claymont DE 19703

Call Sign: N1FLU
Joseph J Petro Jr
2912 Philadelphia Pike
C-2
Claymont DE 19703

Call Sign: KB3VYG
Edward W Carson Jr
146 S Shelley Dr
Claymont DE 19703

Call Sign: KD3HE
Harry Gross
4013 Society Dr
Claymont DE 19703

Call Sign: KB3PRY
Carole L Barrett
4022 Society Dr

Claymont DE 19703

Call Sign: KA3OCI
Monica J Johnson
16 Virginia Ave
Claymont DE 19703

Call Sign: KC3AM
David J Stepnowski
735 W Birchtree Ln
Claymont DE 19703

Call Sign: KB3VNL
Michael A Loveland
2601 Wilson Ave
Claymont DE 19703

Call Sign: KB3ONW
Brandywine Radio Club
Claymont DE 19703

Call Sign: KS3D
Brandywine Radio Club
Claymont DE 19703

Call Sign: N3JJA
James N Nuytens
Claymont DE 19703

Call Sign: W3ZQZ
James Wilkins III
Claymont DE 19703

Call Sign: KJ3N
James N Nuytens
Claymont DE 19703

FCC Amateur Radio License in Clayton

Call Sign: N3ZFO
Mark B Carlson
1532 Alley Corner Rd
Clayton DE 19938

Call Sign: KA2MXN
Roy F Clark Sr
Box 341-1 Rd 126
Clayton DE 19938

Call Sign: N3XQR
Charles Robinson
72 Chance Rd
Clayton DE 19938

Call Sign: N3KBT
Preston L Knight
203 Clayton Ave
Clayton DE 19938

Call Sign: N3YTH
Morris J Haviland
201 Heather Dr
Clayton DE 19938

Call Sign: WB3J
James B Hopkins
129 Hutchison Dr
Clayton DE 19938

Call Sign: N3QXK
Kiyoshi Mc Comb
434 Jordan Dr
Clayton DE 19938

Call Sign: KB3JPH
Jeffrey G Tweed
4574 Judith Rd
Clayton DE 199382844

Call Sign: WW1S
Robert E Botsford
296 Massey Branch Rd
Clayton DE 19938

Call Sign: N3HTT
Kevin G Conway Sr
3032 Millington Rd
Clayton DE 19938

Call Sign: N2BH
Gerald W Smith
946 Saltere Rd
Clayton DE 199383113

Call Sign: N3SUY
Steven D Chillas
203 Smyrna Ave
Clayton DE 19938

Call Sign: KB3NFH
Brian K Shell
202 Sunrise Dr
Clayton DE 19938

Call Sign: KB3PTX
Kenneth L Mcvicker
365 Winnow Dr
Clayton DE 19938

**FCC Amateur Radio
License in Cliffside Park**

Call Sign: KB2YML
Phillip R Cassese
95 Dove Dr
Cliffside Park DE 19958

**FCC Amateur Radio
License in Dagsboro**

Call Sign: KA3BNS
Lewis G Reeves Jr
Box 110 D
Dagsboro DE 19939

Call Sign: N3HNT
Handy J Harris
Box 202 A
Dagsboro DE 19939

Call Sign: N3UFG
Wayne L Brittingham
Box 206
Dagsboro DE 19939

Call Sign: KB3OMQ
Jeffrey S Cook
32140 Canal St
Dagsboro DE 19939

Call Sign: KB3OWS
Jeffrey S Cook
32140 Canal St
Dagsboro DE 19939

Call Sign: KB3HBC
John B Downing
32365 Cea Dag Ct Unit
705
Dagsboro DE 19939

Call Sign: W3PX
James W Smirk
128 Creekside Dr
Dagsboro DE 19939

Call Sign: WA3FYS
Ruley F Banks Jr
28272 Dagsboro Rd
Dagsboro DE 19939

Call Sign: W3FYS
Ruley F Banks Jr
28272 Dagsboro Rd
Dagsboro DE 19939

Call Sign: KB3HI
Gerald J Furman
9 Hiawatha Blvd
Dagsboro DE 19939

Call Sign: N3HKB
Helen L Furman
9 Hiawatha Blvd
Blackwater Village
Dagsboro DE 19939

Call Sign: W3MSG
Gerald J Furman

9 Hiawatha Blvd
Blackwater Village
Dagsboro DE 19939

Call Sign: KA3LEA
Francis F Rickards III
8 Linn Woods Ln
Dagsboro DE 19939

Call Sign: W3HZT
Harold W Hebel
32286 S Dogwood Rd
Dagsboro DE 19939

Call Sign: KE3YD
Milton L Derrickson II
200 Sandy Beach Dr
Dagsboro DE 19939

Call Sign: N3WAU
Brad L Derrickson
200 Sandy Beach Dr
Dagsboro DE 19939

Call Sign: K3GI
Milton L Derrickson II
200 Sandy Beach Dr
Dagsboro DE 19939

Call Sign: K3GKI
Michael S Bass
29733 Sawmill Dr
Dagsboro DE 19939

Call Sign: N3OQH
Denis G Mc Mahon
606 St Andrews Ct
Dagsboro DE 199399234

Call Sign: WA3DZY
Edward G Wilson
34442 Sylvan Vue Dr
Dagsboro DE 19939

Call Sign: KB3NXQ

John F Timmons
30360 Thorogoods Rd
Dagsboro DE 19939

Call Sign: N3XQX
Gregory E Menoche
25732 Timmons Ln
Dagsboro DE 19939

Call Sign: KA3KZQ
Robert J Tyson Mr.
30805 Trails End Dr
Dagsboro DE 19939

Call Sign: KB3WUF
Steve W Benton
202 W Manor Dr
Dagsboro DE 19939

FCC Amateur Radio License in Delaware City

Call Sign: N3OGZ
John F Hughto
110 Clark Cir
Delaware City DE 19706

Call Sign: KB3LLJ
Daryl C Phipps
Delaware City DE 19706

Call Sign: KB3YHI
Kevin P Mcdonough
Delaware City DE 19706

FCC Amateur Radio License in Delmar

Call Sign: KA3NTV
Ralph E Newberry
14740 Baker Rd
Delmar DE 19940

Call Sign: N3NKK
Carol L Newberry

14740 Baker Rd
Delmar DE 19940

Call Sign: K3ZZT
Herbert D Burbage Sr
Box 134
Delmar DE 19940

Call Sign: KA3OTL
George W Sparrow Jr
Box 33
Delmar DE 199409604

Call Sign: W3BAV
Robert F Mack
Box 37
Delmar DE 19940

Call Sign: N3ZOP
Melanie S Chesonis
Box 472B
Delmar DE 199409743

Call Sign: KA3UYJ
Lorie J Gordon
Box 480
Delmar DE 19940

Call Sign: N3XAF
Tracy C Revel
36567 Brittingham Rd
Delmar DE 19940

Call Sign: N3XAH
Gary C Revel
36567 Brittingham Rd
Delmar DE 19940

Call Sign: KA3IFZ
Steven E Franklin
11809 Buckingham Dr
Delmar DE 19940

Call Sign: KB3JGN
Ralph D Merrill Sr

37280 Carr Blvd
Delmar DE 19940

Call Sign: W3RDM
Ralph D Merrill Sr
37280 Carr Blvd
Delmar DE 19940

Call Sign: WA3RFO
Charles M Truitt
Delmar Manor
Delmar DE 19940

Call Sign: KB3PQB
Joanne M Schramm
8287 Delmar Rd
Delmar DE 19940

Call Sign: KB3PQE
Matthew P Schramm
8287 Delmar Rd
Delmar DE 19940

Call Sign: KB3PQD
Toby J Schramm
8287 Delmar Rd
Delmar DE 19940

Call Sign: W3AAB
Brooklyn Park Amateur
Radio Society
403 E State St
Delmar DE 199401254

Call Sign: WQ3N
Brooklyn Park Amateur
Radio Society
403 E State St
Delmar DE 199401254

Call Sign: N3KOX
Anthony P Cucinotta
607 E State St
Delmar DE 19940

Call Sign: W3ECU
Richard H Lehr
403 E State St
Delmar DE 199401254

Call Sign: W3EK
Richard H Lehr
403 E State St
Delmar DE 199401254

Call Sign: AA3SF
John D Price
10314 Francis St
Delmar DE 19940

Call Sign: KB3EZD
Gordon O Brown
701 Grove St
Delmar DE 19940

Call Sign: KB3WZZ
Norman H Willin III
36526 Old Stage Rd
Delmar DE 19940

Call Sign: KA3BML
William H Nichols
7376 Pine Branch Rd
Delmar DE 19940

Call Sign: KB3NRE
Chris Littleton
37054 Robin Hood Rd
Delmar DE 19940

Call Sign: KB3RVO
Edward J Michelsen
38131 St George Rd
Delmar DE 19940

Call Sign: KB3JGC
Philip A Gordon
8149 W Line Rd
Delmar DE 19940

Call Sign: KB3JYW
Philip A Gordon
8149 W Line Rd
Delmar DE 19940

Call Sign: N3LNB
William V Nutter Jr
8227 W Line Rd
Delmar DE 19940

Call Sign: NF3N
Walter E Gordon
8149 W Line Rd
Delmar DE 19940

Call Sign: W3MOM
Robert W Yeadt
8701 Waller Rd
Delmar DE 19940

Call Sign: W3WD
Robin W Yeadt
8735 Waller Rd
Delmar DE 19940

Call Sign: N3KBW
Mary L Bridge
4663 White Deer Rd
Delmar DE 19940

Call Sign: WW3I
William D Bridge
4663 White Deer Rd
Delmar DE 19940

Call Sign: KB3KWU
Irene A Bridge
4663 White Deer Rd
Delmar DE 19940

Call Sign: AB3HD
Irene A Bridge
4663 White Deer Rd
Delmar DE 19940

Call Sign: N3XAG
Craig M Lamond
14808 Whitesville Rd
Delmar DE 199404258

Call Sign: N3FIF
Richard W Malone
38642 Woodside Ct
Delmar DE 19940

FCC Amateur Radio License in Dewey Beach

Call Sign: KA3GRQ
William H Rutherford Jr
18 Chicago St
Dewey Beach DE 19971

Call Sign: W3BSY
Michael E Overman
9 Draper Dr
Dewey Beach DE 19971

FCC Amateur Radio License in Dover

Call Sign: WB2RRE
James A Phillips
2nd Ave
Dover DE 19901

Call Sign: KB3CTM
Mark A Fels
9803 Bay Side Sr
Dover DE 19901

Call Sign: KB3WPA
Phillip A Lane
857 Bison Rd
Dover DE 19904

Call Sign: K3EWI
Phillip A Lane
857 Bison Rd
Dover DE 19904

Call Sign: N3AYK
Brenda G Erdell
Box 318
Dover DE 19901

Call Sign: WA3JMN
Francis H Erdell
Box 318
Dover DE 19901

Call Sign: KA3SBQ
Michael W Dellinger
Box 758
Dover DE 19901

Call Sign: N3WDN
Michael S Smith
104 Brookfield
Dover DE 19901

Call Sign: N3NLT
Edmund S Lucas
101 Brookfield Dr
Dover DE 19901

Call Sign: K4CHE
Breckinridg S Smith
104 Brookfield Dr
Dover DE 19901

Call Sign: KE4MSL
James G Curtis Jr
634 Brookfield Dr
Dover DE 199016537

Call Sign: KA3JTV
John A Balcerak
935 Buck Dr
Dover DE 19901

Call Sign: N3VXJ
Matthew J Pennell
400 Bushy Tail Ln
Dover DE 19904

Call Sign: KA1DWX
Gordon F Durk
115 Carnoustie Rd
Dover DE 19904

Call Sign: K2HVN
William L Jansen
1530 Central Church Rd
Dover DE 19904

Call Sign: KB3UYF
Richard D Cooper Jr
807 Chestnut Grove Rd
Dover DE 199041530

Call Sign: K1CTB
Christopher T Bielecki
7046 Coconut Ct
Dover DE 19901

Call Sign: KA3HYU
Robert A Bonniwell
170 Cooper Rd
Dover DE 19901

Call Sign: NY3R
William A Colom Sr
527 Crawford Ave
Dover DE 19901

Call Sign: WB7FDX
Paul W Ford Jr
44 Deborah Dr
Dover DE 19901

Call Sign: KB3TTY
Manuel J Velasquez
568 Dinahs Corner Rd
Dover DE 19904

Call Sign: KB0FQU
R Larry Nance
411 Dogwood Ave
Dover DE 19904

Call Sign: N3KH
Kenneth H Smith
4 Dogwood Ct
Dover DE 199044809

Call Sign: N3YRT
Sean M Huber
10 Dogwood Ct
Dover DE 19904

Call Sign: KB9YBF
Raymond E Harris
22 Duchess Cir
Dover DE 19901

Call Sign: N3BPS
George H Badell
580 Dundee Rd
Dover DE 19904

Call Sign: KB3CUT
Gordon W Street
658 Dyke Branch Rd
Dover DE 19901

Call Sign: KB3UKD
Janet L Crandall
539 E Loockerman St
Dover DE 19901

Call Sign: WA3WIS
Veronica C Balcerak
728 E Loockerman St
Dover DE 19901

Call Sign: WB3HSP
David J Balcerak
728 E Loockerman St
Dover DE 19901

Call Sign: N3HLS
Richard J Kosior
12 Elm Terrace
Dover DE 19901

Call Sign: WB0EQ
John F Sehring
47 Elm Terrace Co
Vandorpe
Dover DE 19901

Call Sign: KB3PIY
John L Pancoast
176 Evergreen Dr
Dover DE 19901

Call Sign: N3LHQ
William J Trentacoste
509 Fairview Ave
Dover DE 19904

Call Sign: KB3NRR
Ronald E Waid Jr
540 Fairview Ave
Dover DE 19904

Call Sign: K3REW
Ronald E Waid Jr
540 Fairview Ave
Dover DE 19904

Call Sign: N3HRK
Joel M Rutenberg
2 Fairway Ct
Dover DE 19904

Call Sign: WP4LEM
Jerry Oscar Velazquez
Sanabria
1300 Farmview Dr Apt M-24
Dover DE 19904

Call Sign: KB3WKT
Amanda M Horton
161 Fawn Haven Walk
Dover DE 19901

Call Sign: KB3WIV

Robert A Bell
106 Fieldcrest Dr
Dover DE 19904

Call Sign: WB3AYE
Walter W Winazak
2024 Forrest Ave
Dover DE 19904

Call Sign: N3TWC
Angelo L Albarran Sr
3411 Forrest Ave
Dover DE 19904

Call Sign: KF4KCQ
Robert J Mc Kennett
108 Fox Hall Dr
Dover DE 19904

Call Sign: KG4CJI
Robert J Mckennett Sr
108 Fox Hall Dr
Dover DE 19904

Call Sign: W3RYQ
Donald F Tinari
302 Fox Pointe Dr
Dover DE 19904

Call Sign: KB3WUS
James N Combs
102 Gagen Ct
Dover DE 19904

Call Sign: KB3JFZ
Bill J Morrow
406 Great Geneva Dr
Dover DE 19901

Call Sign: KB0JJN
William P Harshman
143 Greenhill Ave
Dover DE 199014218

Call Sign: KB3QKC

Robert A Mccleary
6 Greenview Dr
Dover DE 199015744

Call Sign: KB3UAZ
Robert A Mccleary
6 Greenview Dr
Dover DE 199015744

Call Sign: KB3KIS
Paul M Huebner Jr
60 Greenview Dr
Dover DE 19901

Call Sign: KF6IWB
Virna Liz B Martin
163 Hampton Dr
Dover DE 19904

Call Sign: N9VBO
Daniel R Vorbau
338 Hiawatha Ln
Dover DE 19904

Call Sign: N3ZPA
Mark T Mondell
116 Hiawatha Ln
Dover DE 19904

Call Sign: KB3MHQ
John E Harman
215 Jefferson Terrace
Dover DE 19904

Call Sign: KB3MHP
Kirk E Golden
215 Jefferson Terrace
Dover DE 19904

Call Sign: N3FZP
Sonny Z Postles
3258 Kenton Rd
Dover DE 19904

Call Sign: W3YQW

Jonathan S Willis III
3868 Kenton Rd
Dover DE 19904

Call Sign: WB3BXC
Bernard J Kappe
4753 Kenton Rd
Dover DE 19904

Call Sign: N4EVX
Jeff A Rakes
25 Liberty Dr
Dover DE 19904

Call Sign: N3RSO
Robert W Boleslawski
112 Logan Dr
Dover DE 19901

Call Sign: N3GAO
John R De Lauder
33 Lotus St
Dover DE 19901

Call Sign: K3LT
Lawrence J Roll
200 Mahogany Pl
Dover DE 199019272

Call Sign: W3DOV
Dover Amateur Radio
Club
200 Mahogany Pl
Dover DE 199019272

Call Sign: N3YVS
Robert L Mc Clements
11 Maple Ln
Dover DE 199046021

Call Sign: W3OWM
Edward W Smitheman
34 Maple Ln
Dover DE 19901

Call Sign: N3KQO
Thomas M Penders
7 Mc Bry Ct
Dover DE 19901

Call Sign: WA3JJL
Hugo V Tjinkonfat
931 Mc Dowell Dr
Dover DE 19901

Call Sign: KA3JPJ
Brooks M Bartlett
1175 Mckee Rd Apt 201
Dover DE 19904

Call Sign: KE3UY
Mark B Holloway Sr
56 Meadow Ridge
Parkway
Dover DE 19904

Call Sign: KB3UFJ
Richard A Kirby
349 Memory Ln
Dover DE 19901

Call Sign: WA3KXV
Mark D Garrett
4 Michael Ct
Dover DE 19904

Call Sign: KB3JGA
Thomas M Pomponio
31 Mifflin Rd
Dover DE 19904

Call Sign: W2SGP
Merton T Lucas Sr
703 Miller Dr
Dover DE 19901

Call Sign: N3FWZ
David P Dowty
82 Mitscher Rd
Dover DE 19901

Call Sign: KA3ZJV
Hugh R Dale
953 Monroe Ter
Dover DE 19901

Call Sign: KB3RKO
Samuel G Cannan
200 N Bay Dr
Dover DE 19901

Call Sign: WB3AOG
Richard J Kobza
223 N Bradford St
Dover DE 19901

Call Sign: KB3KPJ
Anne Frances Goodrich
229 N Bradford St
Dover DE 19904

Call Sign: N1PXU
Michael A Kirkpatrick
120 N State St
Dover DE 199013875

Call Sign: N3PMD
Andre Watson
New York Ln
Dover DE 19901

Call Sign: KB3PQF
Ronald K Siebach
16 Oakcrest Dr
Dover DE 19901

Call Sign: N3FSU
Charles D Wilson Jr
142 Old Forge Dr
Dover DE 19904

Call Sign: W3SPL
Frederick V Tarburton
108 Old Mill Rd
Dover DE 19901

Call Sign: KB3GFN
Kimberly A Mattinson
30 Old Rudnick Ln
Dover DE 19901

Call Sign: KB3GFO
Michael Mattinson
30 Old Rudnick Ln
Dover DE 19901

Call Sign: W3MD
Joseph F Andrews
10 Owen David Ct
Dover DE 19904

Call Sign: KB3PFE
Christopher Andrews
10 Owen David Ct
Dover DE 19904

Call Sign: KB3MOT
Jonathan P Andrews
10 Owen David Ct
Dover DE 19904

Call Sign: N3WQY
Ricardo J Lucas
P O Box 960
Dover DE 19903

Call Sign: N3WON
Thomas E Henry Sr
120 Parkers Dr
Dover DE 19904

Call Sign: KB3LWC
Walter L Parsons Jr
7395 Pearsons Corner Rd
Dover DE 19904

Call Sign: AA3IQ
Ignace Kosmac
1441 Persimmon Tree Ln
Dover DE 19901

Call Sign: WB3ITG
Richard M Wandall Jr
449 Pickering Beach Rd
Dover DE 199017141

Call Sign: KA3EOW
Russell L Hersh
155 Pine Cone Dr
Dover DE 199011966

Call Sign: KB3HIV
Patrick J Malloy
62 Pine Valley Rd
Dover DE 19904

Call Sign: N3CYZ
Ralph B Hinzman Jr
62 Pleasanton Dr
Dover DE 19901

Call Sign: W3HZW
Kent County Amateur
Radio Club
911 Public Safety Blvd
Dover DE 19901

Call Sign: N3LOD
Nathaniel Gibbs Jr
234 Red Tail Dr
Dover DE 199045562

Call Sign: W2GPY
Allen E Hall
27 Richardson Cir
Dover DE 199016311

Call Sign: N2IBU
Brett L Bivens
590 Roberta Ave
Dover DE 19901

Call Sign: K3WCO
Brett L Bivens
590 Roberta Ave

Dover DE 19901

Call Sign: KB3KFO
Heather M Bivens
590 Roberta Ave
Dover DE 19901

Call Sign: N3GLM
Lowell E Rowe Jr
421 Ross St
Dover DE 19901

Call Sign: KE3ST
Eugene A Legrand
1 S Dayflower Ct
Dover DE 19904

Call Sign: WW3E
Robert W Baker
184 S Fairfield Dr
Dover DE 19901

Call Sign: N3YRS
James B Brewer Jr
108 S Governers Ave Apt
1
Dover DE 19904

Call Sign: KA1FYL
Jonathan Patz
2 S Nace Ln
Dover DE 19901

Call Sign: N3WCB
Daniel L Clay
732 S Old Mill Rd
Dover DE 19901

Call Sign: KB3SKG
Daniel L Taylor
71 S Shore Dr
Dover DE 19901

Call Sign: WA4JRZ
Wilbur W Bubb

255 S Shore Dr
Dover DE 19901

Call Sign: KB3JYI
Asher Carey
1371 S State St
Dover DE 19901

Call Sign: N3SKJ
Tracy L Godfrey
424 S State St
Dover DE 19901

Call Sign: N3SSW
Shawn P Tolson
1679 S State St Lot 84
Dover DE 19901

Call Sign: WA3UFT
Thomas F Bernard
1679 S State St A20
Dover DE 19901

Call Sign: N3MEX
Larry F Rumbley
1679 S State St Lot A61
Dover DE 19901

Call Sign: WJ3P
Frank W Scott
15 Sandwich Ct
Dover DE 19901

Call Sign: N3RAE
David G Holt
68 Saxton Rd
Dover DE 19901

Call Sign: K3RMZ
William Semonavick
71 Saxton Rd
Dover DE 19901

Call Sign: N3PHC
Michael J Stone

3098 Seven Hickories Rd
Dover DE 19904

Call Sign: N3OAE
Glenn A Latsha
154 Shamrock Ave
Dover DE 19901

Call Sign: KR1X
Richard B Martin
168 Shamrock Ave
Dover DE 19901

Call Sign: KB3WOZ
Henry Coghlan
17 Sherwood Ct
Dover DE 19904

Call Sign: KB3PCZ
State of Delaware
Department of Technology
and Information
801 Silver Lake Blvd
Dover DE 19904

Call Sign: K3DTI
State of Delaware
Department of Technology
and Information
801 Silver Lake Blvd
Dover DE 19904

Call Sign: KB3TVS
Edward D Haas Jr
1168 Sorghum Mill Rd
Dover DE 19901

Call Sign: AB3KR
Edward D Haas Jr
1168 Sorghum Mill Rd
Dover DE 19901

Call Sign: N3QGZ
John K Boland II
129 Springfield Way

Dover DE 19901

Call Sign: N3QJN
John K Boland III
129 Springfield Way
Dover DE 19901

Call Sign: K3JKB
John K Boland II
129 Springfield Way
Dover DE 19901

Call Sign: N3OHT
Justin Van Winkle
3710 B Spruce St
Dover DE 19901

Call Sign: KB3TLC
William A Kurlander
266 Stone Ridge Dr
Dover DE 19901

Call Sign: N3WAK
William A Kurlander
266 Stone Ridge Dr
Dover DE 19901

Call Sign: KB3USH
Robert J Varipapa Sr
101 Stuart Dr
Dover DE 19901

Call Sign: KB3VCQ
Serg Koren
206 Topaz Cir
Dover DE 19904

Call Sign: KA3BDG
John H Morrison
67 Upland Ave
Dover DE 19901

Call Sign: KB3RIW
Cubbage Brown Jr
3263 Upper King Rd

Dover DE 19904

Call Sign: K7VSW
Vernon S Webb Jr
3263 Upper King Rd
Dover DE 19904

Call Sign: N3WAT
Steven D Gomolski
3660 Upper King Rd
Dover DE 19904

Call Sign: AB2UU
Vincent F Pisano
89 Verona Ct
Dover DE 19904

Call Sign: N3KKO
George R Truitt
1265 Victory Chapel Rd
Dover DE 19904

Call Sign: K3WO
George R Truitt
1265 Victory Chapel Rd
Dover DE 19904

Call Sign: WA3END
Timothy A Spong
317 W Division St
Dover DE 199043228

Call Sign: NF1B
James J Guarino
35 W Huntington Cir
Dover DE 19904

Call Sign: N1ALK
Kenneth M Lockerby
32 W Loockerman St
Dover DE 19901

Call Sign: AB3HP
Jerry Oscar Velazquez
Sanabria

169 W Sheldrake Cir
Dover DE 19904

Call Sign: N3NOY
Kathleen P Biter
320 Walker Rd
Dover DE 19901

Call Sign: N3NVP
Carol L Biter
320 Walker Rd
Dover DE 19901

Call Sign: N3NVQ
Alice M Biter
320 Walker Rd
Dover DE 19901

Call Sign: NS3E
Edward D Biter Jr
320 Walker Rd
Dover DE 19904

Call Sign: KC3XI
Charles E Fazekas
1026 Walnut Shade Rd
Dover DE 19901

Call Sign: KA3NGU
Gary E Emeigh
206 Webbs Ln
Dover DE 19904

Call Sign: KB3AJP
Daniel P Statuti
539 West St
Dover DE 19901

Call Sign: WB3AXX
Dennis F Wootten
1025 Westview Ter
Dover DE 19901

Call Sign: K3NYG
Sandra P Wootten

1025 Westview Ter
Dover DE 19904

Call Sign: KB3ADK
Richard G Lawson
Whiteoak Rd
Dover DE 19901

Call Sign: K3JP
John L Penrod
922 Wilson Dr
Dover DE 19904

Call Sign: N3KXW
Felton C Adams Jr
208 Winterberry Dr
Dover DE 19904

Call Sign: N3GF
Gerald P Foss
212 Winterberry Dr
Dover DE 199044818

Call Sign: KD4VLN
Edward L Nowik III
841 Woodcrest Dr
Dover DE 19904

Call Sign: KA3KCS
Clarence W Mc Kinney Jr
48 Woodford St Dupont
Manor
Dover DE 19901

Call Sign: KA3KCT
Janice D Mc Kinney
722 Woodford St Dupont
Manor
Dover DE 19901

Call Sign: KB3NPZ
James M Caine
Dover DE 19903

Call Sign: W3CMM

James M Caine
Dover DE 19903

Call Sign: KB3WPB
Margot A Brennan
Dover DE 19903

Call Sign: N3HPP
Mark A Peterson
Box 51685
Dover AFB DE 19902

Call Sign: KB3YFZ
Matthew Hansen
435 Chevron Ave 242
Dover AFB DE 19902

Call Sign: N3ZVD
Timothy M Dean
Box 386
Ellendale DE 19941

Call Sign: KB3OFZ
George M Lewis Jr
12841 Piney Branch Rd
Ellendale DE 19941

Call Sign: KA3CDF
Lars R Spencer
12862 Piney Branch Rd
Ellendale DE 19941

Call Sign: NS3F
Lars R Spencer
12862 Piney Branch Rd
Ellendale DE 19941

Call Sign: K3GF
Glenn J Friedenreich

22182 Reynolds Pond Rd
Ellendale DE 19941

Call Sign: KB3JBW
Branden M Reed
17129 Webbs Rd
Ellendale DE 19941

Call Sign: KA3TXC
Joseph D Morris
1219 Maple Ave
Elsmere DE 19805

Call Sign: KB3PMT
William D Stephey Jr
8 Tamarack Ave
Elsmere DE 19805

Call Sign: N3HPA
Robert A Speakman Jr
2515 Andrews Lake Rd
Felton DE 19943

Call Sign: WB3EUR
Rosalie L Speakman
2515 Andrews Lake Rd
Felton DE 19943

Call Sign: KB3RKP
Richard R Reynolds
89 Barbara Blvd
Felton DE 19943

Call Sign: K3ELK
Richard R Reynolds
89 Barbara Blvd
Felton DE 199435736

Call Sign: WA3CTL

Raymond J Stone
1053 Barratts Chapel Rd
Felton DE 19943

Call Sign: K3LGC
Donald M Babyok
1693 Barratts Chapel Rd
Felton DE 199435317

Call Sign: K3RTN
H Earl Roberts
Box 239
Felton DE 19943

Call Sign: K3GZZ
Bruce E Straw Sr
Box 595
Felton DE 19943

Call Sign: KB3VXX
John K Feeney
862 Campground Rd
Felton DE 19943

Call Sign: K3JLY
Robert A Speakman
5614 Canterbury Rd
Felton DE 19943

Call Sign: N3EJS
Charles K Pitts Jr
9410 Canterbury Rd
Felton DE 199435552

Call Sign: KB3TTZ
Mark F Letavish
389 Charles Ct
Felton DE 19943

Call Sign: KB3SVU
Diane L Acker
194 Charlies Ct
Felton DE 19943

Call Sign: KB3RDW

Carl F Acker
194 Charlies Ct
Felton DE 19943

Call Sign: K3CFA
Carl F Acker
194 Charlies Ct
Felton DE 19943

Call Sign: KA3VAR
Shawn E Cooper
County Rd 283
Felton DE 19943

Call Sign: KA3VAS
Larry G Thompson Sr
County Rd 283
Felton DE 19943

Call Sign: N3IOC
Tony J Tyler
4277 Hills Market Rd
Felton DE 19943

Call Sign: KB3VSX
John D Spickes
5067 Hopkins Cemetery
Rd
Felton DE 19943

Call Sign: KO3I
John D Spickes
5067 Hopkins Cemetery
Rd
Felton DE 19943

Call Sign: KB3VSW
Rose L Spickes
5067 Hopkins Cemetery
Rd
Felton DE 19943

Call Sign: W3OOL
Rose L Spickes

5067 Hopkins Cemetery
Rd
Felton DE 19943

Call Sign: KB3QCQ
Cody W Garland
5283 Hopkins Cemetery
Rd
Felton DE 19943

Call Sign: W5CWG
Cody W Garland
5283 Hopkins Cemetery
Rd
Felton DE 19943

Call Sign: AA1K
Jon P Zaimes
3765 Midstate Rd
Felton DE 19943

Call Sign: AB1P
Jeanette M S Zaimes
3765 Midstate Rd
Felton DE 19943

Call Sign: WA2FPK
William A Hering
108 N Erin Ave
Felton DE 19943

Call Sign: W3YS
William A Hering
108 N Erin Ave
Felton DE 19943

Call Sign: KB3HTG
Kristina L Dunn
118 Oaknoll Ave
Felton DE 19943

Call Sign: KA2AAQ
Thomas J Cleary Jr
134 Paris Ln
Felton DE 19943

Call Sign: KA2EUJ
Karen G Cleary
134 Paris Ln
Felton DE 19943

Call Sign: KB3BVI
Justin C Mcconnell
811 Peach Basket Rd
Felton DE 19943

Call Sign: AA3JM
William M Mc Connell
811 Peachbasket Rd
Felton DE 19943

Call Sign: W3CKH
Gary B Homewood
12497 S Dupont Hwy
Felton DE 19943

Call Sign: N3THU
Robert L Walker
12328 S Dupont Hwy
Felton DE 19943

Call Sign: KB3QIT
Harry L Williams Sr
231 S Ember Dr
Felton DE 19943

Call Sign: N2LOM
John M Connelly Jr
4820 Sandtown Rd
Felton DE 19943

Call Sign: K3GRT
George R Truitt Jr
5665 Sandtown Rd
Felton DE 19943

Call Sign: N3XBM
Stanley W Von Essen Jr
1600 Turkey Point Rd
Felton DE 19943

Call Sign: KB3PMM
Christopher J Wolfe Sr
73 Vineward Ln
Felton DE 19943

Call Sign: KB3DGH
Carolyn M Blazejowski
105 W Sewell St
Felton DE 19943

Call Sign: KC3OQ
Robert L Reinhardt
1148 Willow Grove Rd
Felton DE 199432909

Call Sign: WB3ILS
Paul D Mullins
7 Windward Dr
Felton DE 199439639

Call Sign: N3YMS
Nicholas Fedirko
107 Winfred Dr
Felton DE 19943

Call Sign: KA3SIZ
George R Truitt Jr
Felton DE 19943

Call Sign: N3BUH
Paul K Tuley
Felton DE 199430456

Call Sign: KB3UTZ
Susan L Truitt
Felton DE 19943

FCC Amateur Radio License in Fenwick Island

Call Sign: KB3MDZ
Christopher D Pridgeon
1 E James St

Fenwick Island DE 19944

Call Sign: KB3PGF
Dennett E Pridgeon
1 E James St
Fenwick Island DE 19944

FCC Amateur Radio License in Frankford

Call Sign: KA3NZY
Irwin R Saulsbury
Box 230-7 Rd 2
Frankford DE 19945

Call Sign: KB3JBP
George A Skiba
Box 63
Frankford DE 19945

Call Sign: N3KIQ
Robert A Miskin
Box 86C
Frankford DE 19945

Call Sign: N3WYJ
Charles W Daisey
24476 Cypress Rd
Frankford DE 19945

Call Sign: KB3DYE
Pauline C Daisey
24193 Daisey
Frankford DE 199459544

Call Sign: WA3CZO
Walter E Reim
199 Monterray Ave
Frankford DE 19945

Call Sign: KB3IWV
Keith E Murray
32981 Murray Rd
Frankford DE 19945

Call Sign: KB3UJU
Thomas L Raithel
24682 Nottingham Way
Frankford DE 19945

Call Sign: N3YMA
Troy Lc Mc Cabe
36398 Old Mill Bridge Rd
Frankford DE 19945

Call Sign: N3YXD
Patricia A Mc Cabe
36398 Old Mill Bridge Rd
Frankford DE 19945

Call Sign: KB3OLB
Ryan I Bedell
35436 Pen Del Ave
Frankford DE 19945

Call Sign: KB3SDH
Michael Dawson
Peppers Corner Rd
Frankford DE 19945

Call Sign: KA3WPB
George E Gooden
Rd 1
Frankford DE 19945

Call Sign: N3IOD
William A Hammond Jr
34628 W Sherwood Dr
Frankford DE 19945

Call Sign: KB3TXQ
Keegan R Moore
32177 West Rd
Frankford DE 19945

Call Sign: KB3JBV
Lemuel R Collins III
Frankford DE 19945

FCC Amateur Radio
License in Frederica

Call Sign: N3TTT
Adam J Zaimes
4434 Andrews Lake Rd
Frederica DE 19946

Call Sign: KB3MZG
Stephanie R Sestito
7361 Carpenters Bridge Rd
Frederica DE 19946

Call Sign: N3FBI
Stephanie R Sestito
7361 Carpenters Bridge Rd
Frederica DE 19946

Call Sign: WB3ILO
Donald E Driskill
7414 Carpenters Bridge Rd
Frederica DE 199462087

Call Sign: N3UBA
Kenneth J Reitsma
426 Highpoint Park
Frederica DE 19946

Call Sign: W3JRH
James R Husfelt
265 Hudson Branch Dr
Frederica DE 199461862

Call Sign: N3QGY
James R Husfelt
265 Hudsons Branch Dr
Frederica DE 199461862

Call Sign: N3WYW
Anna M Husfelt
265 Hudsons Branch Dr
Frederica DE 199461862

Call Sign: KB3LHJ
Robert D Freeman

315 Lorraine Dr
Frederica DE 199461800

Call Sign: KA3IJO
James A Treadway
131 Maple Dr High Point
Trailer Pk
Frederica DE 19946

Call Sign: K0UWO
James L Laws
131 Maple Dr Highpoint
MHP
Frederica DE 199469711

Call Sign: KA3PJP
Sandra L Laws
131 Maple Dr Highpoint
MHP
Frederica DE 19946

Call Sign: KA3MSG
Peggy L Reisinger
28 N Bay Shore Dr
Frederica DE 19946

Call Sign: KC3OO
Timothy A Reisinger
28 N Bay Shore Dr
Frederica DE 19946

Call Sign: K3CHP
Joseph S Mikuckis
45 Ruyter Dr
Frederica DE 199461916

Call Sign: K3KF
Eugene Golabek
Frederica DE 19946

FCC Amateur Radio
License in Georgetown

Call Sign: KB3MZN
George W Headley Jr

21142 Arrow Rd
Georgetown DE 19947

Call Sign: W3LOP
George W Headley Jr
21142 Arrow Rd
Georgetown DE 19947

Call Sign: N3AWP
Bruce C Kahler
Box 134L Rd 322
Georgetown DE 19947

Call Sign: K3ZKD
Richard H Reuling Sr
Box 148E
Georgetown DE 19947

Call Sign: N3YVU
Thomas L Mc Cabe
Box 203 B
Georgetown DE 19947

Call Sign: N2CJK
Elliot N Fruman
Box 327K RR 2
Georgetown DE 19947

Call Sign: N3ZWJ
Louis N Caporaso
Box 56
Georgetown DE 19947

Call Sign: N3LGQ
Harrison E Hammond
9 Bramhall St
Georgetown DE 19947

Call Sign: KA3KZA
Walter H Barcus IV
28244 Bryans Store Rd
Georgetown DE 19947

Call Sign: N3WQB
Donna D Kahler

22119 Bunting Rd
Georgetown DE 19947

Call Sign: KB3PGG
Nicholas R Phillips
6 Chicory Dr
Georgetown DE 19947

Call Sign: KB3RAW
Jonathan A Santon
22518 Concord Pond Rd
Georgetown DE 19947

Call Sign: KB3OBU
Steven J Timmons
22239 Deep Branch Rd
Georgetown DE 19947

Call Sign: W3SJT
Steven J Timmons
22239 Deep Branch Rd
Georgetown DE 19947

Call Sign: K3PFW
John S Ferguson
20116 Donovans Rd
Georgetown DE 19947

Call Sign: KB3HEV
Sussex County Eoc Station
Support Team
20116 Donovans Rd
Georgetown DE 19947

Call Sign: KB3TXW
Avery W Withers
31 Evergreen Dr
Georgetown DE 19947

Call Sign: KB3TXT
Matthew S Oldland
15 Fairway W Dr
Georgetown DE 19947

Call Sign: KB3OLA

Bailey J Elmore
200 Gardner Ave
Georgetown DE 19947

Call Sign: KB3PGA
Charles C Watkins
18 Godwall Dr
Georgetown DE 19947

Call Sign: KB3RPQ
Rodney T Mcgee
26135 Gov Stockley Rd
Georgetown DE 19947

Call Sign: N3LGM
Ronald F Whaley
29526 Jones Store Rd
Georgetown DE 19947

Call Sign: KB3QCR
Leonard R Hecker Jr
22535 Lakeshore Dr
Georgetown DE 19947

Call Sign: K3LRH
Leonard R Hecker Jr
22535 Lakeshore Dr
Georgetown DE 19947

Call Sign: KB3NRV
David Pedersen
316 N Bedford St
Georgetown DE 19947

Call Sign: KB3MJQ
Jeremy D Pedersen
316 N Bedford St
Georgetown DE 19947

Call Sign: AB3DL
Jeremy D Pedersen
316 N Bedford St
Georgetown DE 19947

Call Sign: KB3TXP

Jerry A Mullins
207 N Front St
Georgetown DE 19947

Call Sign: KB3TOJ
Warren B Knowles
21543 Park Ave
Georgetown DE 19947

Call Sign: KB3QFF
Keith I Walls
22383 Park Ave
Georgetown DE 19947

Call Sign: N3QPH
Linda R Mason
19377 Parsons Rd
Georgetown DE 19947

Call Sign: KA3JVL
Walter W Richardson Jr
Patterson Pl
Georgetown DE 19947

Call Sign: KB3HSZ
Bennett J Galvacky
22392 Peterkins Rd
Georgetown DE 19947

Call Sign: KB3SAT
William G Wise Jr
24577 Pie Ln
Georgetown DE 19947

Call Sign: W3WGW
William G Wise Jr
24577 Pie Ln
Georgetown DE 19947

Call Sign: K3JL
John R Low
23161 Raccoon Ditch Rd
Georgetown DE 19947

Call Sign: KB3BHL

Sussex Amateur Radio
Assn
23161 Raccoon Ditch Rd
Georgetown DE 19947

Call Sign: WA3VIT
Barbara A Low
23161 Raccoon Ditch Rd
Georgetown DE 19947

Call Sign: K3RSM
Norman H Johnson
Rd Box 107A
Georgetown DE
199479713

Call Sign: KB3RAV
Ryan P Faucett
222 S Bedford St
Georgetown DE 19947

Call Sign: KB3LHD
William R Leager
237 S Bedford St
Georgetown DE 19947

Call Sign: KA3ZON
Kenneth W Rogers Sr
16421 Seashore Hwy
Georgetown DE 19947

Call Sign: KB3HFT
Kenneth W Rogers Sr
16421 Seashore Hwy
Georgetown DE 19947

Call Sign: K3KWR
Kenneth W Rogers Sr
16421 Seashore Hwy
Georgetown DE 19947

Call Sign: W4OCC
Glenn R Bilger
29 Silver Berry St
Georgetown DE 19947

Call Sign: KI4FYN
Joan L Bilger
29 Silverberry St
Georgetown DE 19947

Call Sign: N3JCF
Dorothy C Sammons
23318 Springfield Rd
Georgetown DE 19947

Call Sign: WA3KZX
Joseph W Schorah
20472 State Forest Rd
Georgetown DE 19947

Call Sign: WA3TFK
Rose M Schorah
20472 State Forest Rd
Georgetown DE 19947

Call Sign: KA3SGF
Bonnie S Low
20520 State Forest Rd
Georgetown DE 19947

Call Sign: KB3OKX
Jonathan P Sharman
111 W Adams St
Georgetown DE 19947

Call Sign: N3YIU
Nelson P Warren Jr
308 W Market St
Georgetown DE
199479628

Call Sign: N3JRB
Thomas L Mc Dougall Sr
18572 Whaleys Corner Rd
Georgetown DE 19947

Call Sign: KB3JUT
Merrill R Baker III
13684 Wilson Hill Rd

Georgetown DE 19947

Call Sign: N3XBI
William S Hamilton 2Nd
15541 Wilson Hill Rd
Georgetown DE 19947

Call Sign: N3XBJ
Lucille R Hamilton
15541 Wilson Hill Rd
Georgetown DE 19947

Call Sign: N3XBL
Minos J Wilson
15541 Wilson Hill Rd
Georgetown DE 19947

Call Sign: KB3WZH
Eric J Evars
200 Wilson St
Georgetown DE 19947

Call Sign: KB3PML
Clifford A Chipman
1 Wood Duck Way
Georgetown DE 19947

Call Sign: KB3HTH
Ryan A Lecates
21796 Zoar Rd
Georgetown DE 19947

Call Sign: KB3KCU
Sussex Tech Amateur
Radio Club
Georgetown DE 19947

Call Sign: K3STR
Sussex Tech Amateur
Radio Club
Georgetown DE 19947

Call Sign: W4PON
Arthur E Sowers
Georgetown DE 19947

Call Sign: KB3FZE
Kelly L Davis
Georgetown DE 19947

Call Sign: KB1EJH
Carl Davis
Georgetown DE
199470180

Call Sign: KB3MJO
Walter L Vanaman
Georgetown DE 19947

FCC Amateur Radio License in Gotha

Call Sign: KF4PWR
Tobias Offhaus
17 W Sylten St
Gotha DE 19867

FCC Amateur Radio License in Greenville

Call Sign: KB6HEL
Christine C Go
4 Carriage Rd
Greenville DE 19807

Call Sign: KB3GVB
Jose D Cedeno
100 Congressional Dr Apt
D
Greenville DE 19807

Call Sign: KB3QKG
H Bruce Hardy
910 Fairthorne Ave
Greenville DE 19807

Call Sign: K3WZT
H Bruce Hardy
910 Fairthorne Ave
Greenville DE 19807

Call Sign: W2AR
Willard L Mc Ewen
4031 Kennett Pike
Greenville DE 19807

Call Sign: N3CJR
Anthony J Brzoska
112 Montchan Dr
Greenville DE 19807

Call Sign: K3AJK
Roy Wall
Senatorial Dr
Greenville DE 19807

Call Sign: WA3FAX
Dorothy T Gold
Snuff Mill Rd Box 3532
Greenville DE 19807

Call Sign: WA3FAW
Harry E Gold
3532 Snuffmill Rd
Greenville DE 19807

Call Sign: KB3IZW
Edmund Martinez
1005 Talon Ln
Greenville DE 19807

Call Sign: KA3ERO
William I Homer
Greenville DE 19807

FCC Amateur Radio License in Greenwood

Call Sign: KB3JUS
Joseph E Bailey
14213 Adamsville Rd
Greenwood DE 19950

Call Sign: N3XBK
Melissa A Lee

12737 Beach Hwy
Greenwood DE 19950

Call Sign: K3NVV
Frank J Murphy
10479 Blacksmithshop Rd
Greenwood DE 19950

Call Sign: KB3AOV
Philip Stewart
Box 165
Greenwood DE 19950

Call Sign: N0TNX
George W Bowers
Box 167C
Greenwood DE 19950

Call Sign: N3QMN
Robert D Davis
Box 21E
Greenwood DE 19950

Call Sign: KB3PGJ
Angela L Carroll - Baker
13840 Dream Haven Ln
Greenwood DE 19950

Call Sign: K3ACB
Angela L Carroll - Baker
13840 Dream Haven Ln
Greenwood DE 19950

Call Sign: KB3PGD
Gregory L Baker Jr
13840 Dream Haven Ln
Greenwood DE 19950

Call Sign: N3EOS
John S Nichols
405 E Market St
Greenwood DE 19950

Call Sign: KB3TXN
Richard M Grant

10382 Fawn Rd
Greenwood DE 19950

Call Sign: N2XKO
William H Wilson Jr
4 Gardeina Blvd
Greenwood DE 19950

Call Sign: KB3NTI
Icannis V Wilson
4 Gardenia Blvd
Greenwood DE 19950

Call Sign: WA3QGO
Daniel T Pawlowski
8 Gardenia Blvd
Greenwood DE 199502501

Call Sign: N3EZI
Robert P Stevenson Sr
11525 Holly Tree Ln
Greenwood DE 19950

Call Sign: N3ZJP
Todd W Boyer
5 Hollyhock Dr
Greenwood DE 19950

Call Sign: KB2KSZ
David P Weaver
8 Hollyhock Dr
Greenwood DE 19950

Call Sign: KA3UGT
Kevin J Drummond
14000 Mile Stretch Rd
Greenwood DE 19950

Call Sign: KB3IWG
William E Xavier
14169 Mile Stretch Rd
Greenwood DE 19950

Call Sign: WA3UAY
Simon L Sharp

14366 Owens Rd
Greenwood DE 19950

Call Sign: KB3HTJ
Ashley L Warnick
14033 Saw Mill Rd
Greenwood DE 19950

Call Sign: N3YDP
Abbey M Carroll
6795 Scotts Store Rd
Greenwood DE 19950

Call Sign: KB3QFI
Jacob E Moore
14273 St Johnston Rd
Greenwood DE 19950

Call Sign: KD3IH
Earl C Radding
12099 Sunset Ln
Greenwood DE 19950

Call Sign: N3EKE
Daniel M Swartzentruber
12505 Victory Ln
Greenwood DE 19950

Call Sign: KB3HTO
Andrew J Creighton
306 W Market
Greenwood DE 19950

Call Sign: N7LXI
Robert E Walker
306 W Market St
Greenwood DE 19950

Call Sign: KD3UI
Hugh H Carroll
13689 Woodbridge Rd
Greenwood DE 19950

Call Sign: W3WAM
Hugh H Carroll

13689 Woodbridge Rd
Greenwood DE 19950

Call Sign: KB3JYH
Grant A Parker
14422 Woodbridge Rd
Greenwood DE 19950

Call Sign: KB3VCP
William J Kuschel
Greenwood DE 19950

Call Sign: AB3MI
William J Kuschel
Greenwood DE 19950

FCC Amateur Radio License in Gwinhurst

Call Sign: W3FJF
J Andrew Moore Sr
2000 Garfield Ave
Gwinhurst DE 198091415

FCC Amateur Radio License in Harbeson

Call Sign: KB3OLD
Jason D Rohlfing
26888 Anderson Corner Rd
Harbeson DE 19951

Call Sign: KB3MXO
John C Murray
27404 Covered Bridge Trl
Harbeson DE 19951

Call Sign: N3LYF
John C Murray
27404 Covered Bridge Trl
Harbeson DE 19951

Call Sign: KB3RAU
Christine N Witke

20801 Doddtown Rd
Harbeson DE 19951

Call Sign: KB3QFH
Tyler C Davidson
22078 Harbeson Rd
Harbeson DE 19947

Call Sign: N3VLR
Chris J Karol
18703 Harbeson Rd
Harbeson DE 19951

Call Sign: WA3IVR
Ralph H Thompson Sr
2 Waterside Ln Pinewater Farm
Harbeson DE 19951

Call Sign: KB3MDX
Walter L Harlow
28658 Woodcrest Dr
Harbeson DE 19951

Call Sign: KB3OBV
Lance K Miller
Harbeson DE 19951

FCC Amateur Radio License in Harrington

Call Sign: N3KBZ
Marie G Green
553 Beebe Rd
Harrington DE 19952

Call Sign: N4NMK
Werner G Schweikert
187 Cams Fortune Way
Harrington DE 19952

Call Sign: N3PG
Barry P Mapp
365 Central Pk Dr
Harrington DE 19952

Call Sign: N3KYA
Edmund R Pajewski
44 Clark St
Harrington DE 199521210

Call Sign: KB3LZZ
Michael Valenti
110 Delaware Ave
Harrington DE 19952

Call Sign: AA3HX
Russell V Ranum Jr
1000 Gingerwood Dr
Harrington DE 19952

Call Sign: K3RVR
Russell V Ranum Jr
1000 Gingerwood Dr
Harrington DE 19952

Call Sign: K3PT
Bobby J Manning
1045 Hammondtown Rd
Harrington DE 19952

Call Sign: KB3VYE
John R Wyatt
415 Harrington Ave
Harrington DE 19952

Call Sign: KB3OJK
Robert P Fries
460 John Hurd Rd
Harrington DE 19952

Call Sign: KA3BDR
John E Block
120 Mechanic St
Harrington DE 19952

Call Sign: KA3LTO
Margaret J Block
120 Mechanic St
Harrington DE 19952

Call Sign: N3TVK
Rex D Evans
7071 Milford-Harrington
Hwy
Harrington DE 19952

Call Sign: N3ZXG
Bradley C Lilly
296 Pleasant Pine Cr
Harrington DE 19952

Call Sign: WA1HQX
Arthur K Carlson Mr
1 Pleasant Pine Ct
Harrington DE 19952

Call Sign: KB3NTQ
Arthur K Carlson Mr
1 Pleasant Pine Ct
Harrington DE 19952

Call Sign: N3STP
Albert T Mason
350 Raughley Hill Rd
Harrington DE 19952

Call Sign: KB3RDV
Albert T Kennedy III
303 S West St
Harrington DE 19952

Call Sign: KB3QFE
Dustin A Miller
12514 Staytonville Rd
Harrington DE 19902

Call Sign: W3ZID
John E Taylor III
500 Two Mile Rd
Harrington DE 19952

Call Sign: N3FLD
Harry P Bolich
7263 Whiteleysburg Rd

Harrington DE 19952

Call Sign: N3WDW
Richard L Mumma
123 Wolcott St
Harrington DE 19952

FCC Amateur Radio License in Hartly

Call Sign: KC2DFP
Gloria M Gross
4405 Arthursville Rd
Hartly DE 19953

Call Sign: WJ3I
James T Telford
4405 Arthursville Rd
Hartly DE 19953

Call Sign: N3ACH
John M Remondi
Box 185
Hartly DE 19953

Call Sign: N3MEM
Dane A Davis
Box 66D Rd 2
Hartly DE 19953

Call Sign: N3ZFN
Franklin J Morgan
63 Brittany Ln
Hartly DE 19953

Call Sign: N3QNA
William A Newton
1828 Everetts Corner Rd
Hartly DE 19953

Call Sign: K3WI
William M Schwartz
190 Gunter Rd
Hartly DE 19953

Call Sign: KA3RCT
Joan A Schwartz
190 Gunter Rd
Hartly DE 199531706

Call Sign: NR3W
James Schwartz
190 Gunter Rd
Hartly DE 199531706

Call Sign: K3JI
James Schwartz
190 Gunter Rd
Hartly DE 199531706

Call Sign: KA3KQO
David A Benini
202 Gunter Rd
Hartly DE 19953

Call Sign: N3EFU
Sharon M Benini
202 Gunter Rd
Hartly DE 19953

Call Sign: KA3VKK
Charles A Shinsky Jr
1439 Hartley Rd
Hartly DE 19953

Call Sign: KB3WYA
David B Storie
645 Hazlettville Rd
Hartly DE 19953

Call Sign: KB3WXZ
Megan L Storie
645 Hazlettville Rd
Hartly DE 19953

Call Sign: KB3DAC
Bruce R Finley
1254 Hourglass Rd
Hartly DE 19953

Call Sign: KB3SLX
David A Gonzalez
198 Pine Tree Rd
Hartly DE 19953

Call Sign: KE3XP
Glenn E Wood
1404 Procters Purchase Rd
Hartly DE 19953

Call Sign: N3XTJ
Christine L Cassidy
1521 Slaughter Station Rd
Hartly DE 19953

Call Sign: W3LSW
Glenn A Seiler
1521 Slaughter Station Rd
Hartly DE 19953

Call Sign: W3DYS
Francis J Dury
949 Tuxward Rd
Hartly DE 19953

Call Sign: N3VQF
Robert J Lahnemann
1285 Tuxward Rd
Hartly DE 19953

Call Sign: N3HZN
Douglas L Aspinwall Sr
5879 Westville Rd
Hartly DE 199532165

Call Sign: N3QJL
Linda S Aspinwall
5879 Westville Rd
Hartly DE 199532615

Call Sign: WB3EOD
John A Funck Jr
Hartly DE 19953

FCC Amateur Radio License in Hockessin

Call Sign: K3BTY
Thomas C Kneavel Jr
7 Arthur Dr
Hockessin DE 19707

Call Sign: WA3YHD
Peter A Jansson
19 Arthur Dr
Hockessin DE 197071012

Call Sign: N3HND
Mark L Mitchell
1 Aston Cir
Hockessin DE 19707

Call Sign: K3ACY
Carl W Thompson III
745 Auburn Mill Rd
Hockessin DE 19707

Call Sign: N3YTI
Anne K H Cleary
825 Benge Rd
Hockessin DE 19707

Call Sign: KA2HCI
John A Mac Evoy
1899 Brackenville Rd
Hockessin DE 19707

Call Sign: KB3FQY
James M Glasow
214 Broadhaven Rd
Hockessin DE 197079538

Call Sign: W3TTQ
James M Glasow
214 Broadhaven Rd
Hockessin DE 197079538

Call Sign: KB3GNI
Jae S Park

750 Brookwood La
Hockessin DE 19707

Call Sign: N3OM
Ron B Mercer
12 Crimson Dr
Hockessin DE 19707

Call Sign: N3ZRS
Barbara K Mercer
12 Crimson Dr
Hockessin DE 197072101

Call Sign: WA3AUP
Kenneth W Lodge
558 Dawson Tract
Hockessin DE 19707

Call Sign: W3KWL
Kenneth W Lodge
558 Dawson Tract
Hockessin DE 19707

Call Sign: KA3SQU
Gerald E Poley Jr
8 Farm House Cir
Hockessin DE 19707

Call Sign: KC5UI
William V Clark
6 Forest Creek Dr
Hockessin DE 19707

Call Sign: KV3U
William E Parsons Jr
113 Highland Dr
Hockessin DE 197079652

Call Sign: KA3UZS
Scott D Zetlan
6 Iron Stone Cir
Hockessin DE 19707

Call Sign: W3HYP
David A Barlow

17 Jacqueline Dr
Hockessin DE 19707

614 Loveville Rd B5C
Hockessin DE 197071605

38 Raphael Rd
Hockessin DE 19707

Call Sign: N3PKU
David G R Short
16 Kent Dr
Hockessin DE 19707

Call Sign: KD3V
David K Fauser Jr
614 Loveville Rd C4A
Hockessin DE 19707

Call Sign: N3VNV
Phillip L Morris
15 Ridgewood Dr
Hockessin DE 19707

Call Sign: W3HIL
John E Boliek
3 Lawlor Ct Rd 3
Hockessin DE 19707

Call Sign: W3STA
Jerome M Krim
614 Loveville Rd E5E
Hockessin DE 19707

Call Sign: N3WEL
Jeffrey P Morris
15 Ridgewood Dr
Hockessin DE 19707

Call Sign: N3RMN
Jose F Gonzalez
737 Letitia Dr
Hockessin DE 19707

Call Sign: K3YQN
Dave I Schonbach
13 Mc Cormick Dr
Hockessin DE 197072107

Call Sign: KA3OIG
Edna O Hackman
505 Runnymede Rd
Hockessin DE 19707

Call Sign: W4IGK
William A Haynes Jr
726 Loveville Rd
Hockessin DE 19707

Call Sign: N3WMN
Nathaniel R Reed
9 Mccormick Dr
Hockessin DE 19707

Call Sign: N3ESY
Elmer E Hackman III
505 Runnymede Rd
Hockessin DE 19707

Call Sign: KA3FCQ
Eleanor V Hoffmann
751 Loveville Rd
Hockessin DE 19707

Call Sign: KB3SLZ
John M Talley
221 Peoples Way
Hockessin DE 19707

Call Sign: KB3VAZ
Ryan M Hickey
102 S Colts Neck Way
Hockessin DE 19707

Call Sign: KD3MQ
Thomas N Hoffmann
751 Loveville Rd
Hockessin DE 19707

Call Sign: N3OMU
Dale V Owen Sr
519 Pershing Rd
Hockessin DE 19707

Call Sign: WA3ZVJ
Francis A Hollweck Jr
344 Shannonbridge Dr
Hockessin DE 19707

Call Sign: N3FLO
Reade Y Tompson
726 Loveville Rd Apt 507
Hockessin DE 197071604

Call Sign: N3OUS
Gary L O Reilly
112 Quaker Hill Ln
Hockessin DE 19707

Call Sign: AD3V
Thomas W Del Pesco
344 Skyline Orchard Dr
Hockessin DE 197079354

Call Sign: WZ3U
Idanna L Peeler
726 Loveville Rd Apt 807
Hockessin DE 197071512

Call Sign: N3RNG
Diane M O Reilly
112 Quaker Hill Ln
Hockessin DE 19707

Call Sign: N2KRU
Scott R Holston
906 Smith St
Hockessin DE 19707

Call Sign: WA3LZS
Jack A Snyder

Call Sign: W9NDZ
Stuart C Lovell

Call Sign: KB3TLQ
Kristen M Roach

40 Stonebridge Dr
Hockessin DE 19707

Call Sign: KB1PPQ
William E Gates
27 Stuyvesant Dr
Hockessin DE 19707

Call Sign: KA3WZM
H Bruce Hardy
412 Topsfield Rd
Hockessin DE 19707

Call Sign: WA3AAS
Michael L Sensor
415 Topsfield Rd
Hockessin DE 19707

Call Sign: N3IGS
Andrew J Greenshields
213 Treetop Ln
Hockessin DE 19707

Call Sign: KA3VGL
Forrest L Sprague
452 Valleybrook Dr
Hockessin DE 19707

Call Sign: KA3VAM
Sreedevi Chittineni
16 Wimbleton Ct
Hockessin DE 19707

Call Sign: KB3HBI
David A Liss
7 Winding Hill Dr
Hockessin DE 19707

Call Sign: KB3IPI
Gerhard R Wittreich
652 Woodview Dr
Hockessin DE 197079665

Call Sign: AB3AA
Gerhard R Wittreich

652 Woodview Dr
Hockessin DE 197079665

Call Sign: N3PL
Gerhard R Wittreich
652 Woodview Dr
Hockessin DE 197079665

Call Sign: KB3VQY
Girard E Hicks
136 Wyeth Way
Hockessin DE 19707

Call Sign: KB3CQO
Mark W Albright
16 York Way
Hockessin DE 19707

Call Sign: WB3AKQ
John O Scales
1 Yorkridge Trl
Hockessin DE 197079633

Call Sign: KA3YWQ
Dale V Owen Jr
Hockessin DE 19707

Call Sign: N9GG
Robert Penneys
Hockessin DE 197070807

Call Sign: WA2TLP
Diana Miller
Hockessin DE 19707

Call Sign: W3AWJ
Hi Tech Rednecks
Hockessin DE 197070807

Call Sign: K3IOK
Hi Tech Rednecks
Hockessin DE 197070807

Call Sign: WU2F
Hi Tech Rednecks

Hockessin DE 197070807

Call Sign: K3HRO
Ham Radio Outlet Of
Delaware Club
Hockessin DE 197070807

Call Sign: W3TT
N E R D S
Hockessin DE 197070807

FCC Amateur Radio License in Houston

Call Sign: KB3PXK
Edward A Nixdorf
267 Broad St
Houston DE 19954

Call Sign: KB3UUA
Lisa T Nixdorf
267 Broad St
Houston DE 19954

Call Sign: KB3TDR
Anibal Rivera
534 Front St
Houston DE 19954

Call Sign: N3RSN
Edward L Trumble Jr
2743 Mesibov Rd
Houston DE 19954

Call Sign: KB3EGL
Keith L Poptanich
211 Minner St
Houston DE 19954

Call Sign: N3PHB
James S Ryals
10 Wharton St
Houston DE 199540215

Call Sign: KB3EAI

Jonathon C Blazejowski
1489 Williamsville Rd
Houston DE 19954

Call Sign: N3KRX
Jerome F Palmer
1489 Williamsville Rd
Houston DE 19954

Call Sign: KB3KFP
Anmarie K Blazejowski
1489 Williamsville Rd
Houston DE 19954

Call Sign: W3AKB
Anmarie K Blazejowski
1489 Williamsville Rd
Houston DE 19954

Call Sign: KB3TJZ
Calvin V Hollis III
4488 Williamsville Rd
Houston DE 19954

Call Sign: AA3ZH
Carolyn M Palmer
1489 Williamsville Rd
Houston DE 19954

FCC Amateur Radio License in Kenton

Call Sign: KC2FUU
Raymond J Lampe Jr
Kenton DE 19956

FCC Amateur Radio License in Laurel

Call Sign: WA3VDJ
David S Fox
30455 Beaver Dam Branch
Rd
Laurel DE 19956

Call Sign: KB3IBK
Jerrold A Fox
30455 Beaver Dam Branch
Rd
Laurel DE 19956

Call Sign: K3ZXP
David T Cretty
30518 Beaver Dam Branch
Rd
Laurel DE 19956

Call Sign: KB3MJP
Lon J Montuori
30483 Beaver Dam Branch
Rd
Laurel DE 19956

Call Sign: KB3QFX
Richard A Bevan Jr
32640 Bi State Blvd
Laurel DE 19956

Call Sign: KB3LEG
Ken Dunn
10055 Birch St
Laurel DE 19956

Call Sign: KB3HTI
Timothy A Messick
32689 Bi-State Blvd
Laurel DE 19956

Call Sign: WA3WBY
Linford L Reynolds
Box 149A
Laurel DE 19956

Call Sign: KB4OYA
Vesta J Jordan
Box 176A
Laurel DE 19956

Call Sign: K3KAE
William L Pedersen

Box 184C
Laurel DE 19956

Call Sign: KB3BBV
Vera P Paulson
Box 190
Laurel DE 19956

Call Sign: WB3FFT
Rodney L Adams
Box 199
Laurel DE 19956

Call Sign: N3WEM
Wesley G Richardson
Box 59
Laurel DE 19956

Call Sign: N3RY
Le Roy F Fasold Jr
119 Broad Creek Rd
Laurel DE 19956

Call Sign: W3PP
E Dallas Carter
28410 Carroll Taylor Dr
Laurel DE 19956

Call Sign: KB3WVD
Carol P Hastings
31166 Chipmans Chase Dr
Laurel DE 19956

Call Sign: AB3IW
Eugene B Hastings Jr
31166 Chipmans Chase Dr
Laurel DE 19956

Call Sign: KB3VYB
Evan K Rogers
11460 Chipmans Pond Rd
Laurel DE 19956

Call Sign: W3FMJ
Evan K Rogers

11460 Chipmans Pond Rd
Laurel DE 19956

Call Sign: KB3JUW
Josh D Kunde
28454 Colonial Rd
Laurel DE 19956

Call Sign: KB3VSV
John P Irelan
11187 County Seat Hwy
Laurel DE 19956

Call Sign: N3WTU
Paul D Barnes
108 Culver
Laurel DE 19956

Call Sign: N3KNT
Rodney G Eikenberry
30808 Dogwood Dr
Broadcreek Estat
Laurel DE 19956

Call Sign: W3KQ
Rick D Jordan
10661 Dorthy Rd
Laurel DE 19956

Call Sign: K3HEN
Vesta J Jordan
10661 Dorthy Rd
Laurel DE 19956

Call Sign: KB3MDY
Lewis P Heck Jr
28216 Dukes Lumber Rd
Laurel DE 19956

Call Sign: N3RRR
Lewis P Heck Jr
28216 Dukes Lumber Rd
Laurel DE 19956

Call Sign: KA3TSC

Robert A Johnson
602 E 4th St
Laurel DE 19956

Call Sign: WB4IBZ
William D O Quin Jr
606 Forest Hill Knoll Dr
Laurel DE 19956

Call Sign: W3WEO
William D O Quin Jr
606 Forest Knoll Dr
Laurel DE 199569400

Call Sign: N3NRQ
Glen D Alexander
43 Hickman Dr
Laurel DE 19956

Call Sign: KB3UUX
Joseph T Yawn
31469 Hitch Pd Rd
Laurel DE 19956

Call Sign: KC2DLC
John P Marinello
31433 Hitch Pond Rd
Laurel DE 19956

Call Sign: KB3LHI
Robert A Johnson
14961 Johnson Rd
Laurel DE 19956

Call Sign: K3EFM
Robert A Johnson
14961 Johnson Rd
Laurel DE 19956

Call Sign: K3MQ
Robert A Johnson
14961 Johnson Rd
Laurel DE 19956

Call Sign: W3RCL

Robert C Landes
14138 Johnson Rd
Laurel DE 19956

Call Sign: KB3DAO
David W Hudson
10811 Kurtz Dr
Laurel DE 19956

Call Sign: W3FXF
David F Edwards Jr
114 Lakeside Dr
Laurel DE 199561144

Call Sign: WA3LLZ
Charles E Swift
109 Lewis Dr
Laurel DE 19956

Call Sign: N3WHB
John F Kenney
136 Locust St
Laurel DE 19956

Call Sign: KE3ZZ
Layton E Timmons
7 Mill Pond
Laurel DE 199561727

Call Sign: KB3RVN
Garrett R Anderson
6890 Millcreek Cir
Laurel DE 19956

Call Sign: N3LZ
John L Hedrick
6428 Millcreek Rd
Laurel DE 19956

Call Sign: N3WET
John L Hedrick
6428 Millcreek Rd
Laurel DE 199569522

Call Sign: KB3IZR

Tapmarc
34087 Old Hickory Rd
Laurel DE 19956

Call Sign: W3DOG
Tapmarc
34087 Old Hickory Rd
Laurel DE 19956

Call Sign: K3TKJ
Alan L Waller
34087 Old Hickory Rd
Laurel DE 19956

Call Sign: N2BJV
Darrel H Smith
31749 Old Hickory Rd
Laurel DE 19956

Call Sign: N2XQ
Nicholas D Pellecchia
4721 Phillips Landing Rd
Laurel DE 19956

Call Sign: KD6DKD
Peter E Short
323 Poplar St Apt 2 S
Laurel DE 19956

Call Sign: N3ZRZ
Daniel M Walczak
16460 Quail Run Dr
Laurel DE 19956

Call Sign: KB3TXO
Anthony Taylor
32561 Samuel Hill Rd
Laurel DE 19956

Call Sign: KB3TXM
Peter J Ottley
3092 Scotland Rd
Laurel DE 19956

Call Sign: KB3UJS

John M Porter
9248 Sharptown
Laurel DE 19956

Call Sign: N3BR
John M Porter
9248 Sharptown
Laurel DE 19956

Call Sign: W3DOG
T Allen Phillips
144 Sharptown Rd
Laurel DE 19956

Call Sign: N3SLX
Paul H Paulson
6990 Shell Bridge Rd
Laurel DE 19956

Call Sign: WA3GGM
Robert L Rickards
35212 Shepherds Path
Laurel DE 199569304

Call Sign: KA3OBV
Albert F Nocar Jr
14748 Shiloh Church Rd
Laurel DE 19956

Call Sign: W3QU
Albert F Nocar Jr
14748 Shiloh Church Rd
Laurel DE 19956

Call Sign: KB3FWM
Paul A Higley
14767 Shiloh Church Rd
Laurel DE 19956

Call Sign: W3HE
Paul A Higley
14767 Shiloh Church Rd
Laurel DE 19956

Call Sign: KB3BMT

James D Hollis
30819 Shiloh Dr
Laurel DE 199562949

Call Sign: KE3T
Layton E Timmons
124 Short Ave
Laurel DE 199561152

Call Sign: KB3CRL
Julia N Blaine
402 Spruce St
Laurel DE 19956

Call Sign: KB3NRF
Brandon Wilkins
34956 Susan Beach Rd
Laurel DE 19956

Call Sign: KB3SDK
Sung H Kang
12834 Taylor Mill Rd
Laurel DE 19956

Call Sign: K3BUG
Russell Horsey Jr
444 W 6th St
Laurel DE 19956

Call Sign: N3HRV
Samuel W Campbell III
103 W 8th St
Laurel DE 19956

Call Sign: KB3DRN
Seaford High School
Amateur Radio Club
908 West St
Laurel DE 199561932

Call Sign: N3WYL
Dona W Blaine
908 West St
Laurel DE 199561932

Call Sign: N3WYM
F Matthew Blaine
908 West St
Laurel DE 199561932

Call Sign: KB3VJU
Aaron L Calloway
36199 Whaleys Rd
Laurel DE 19956

Call Sign: KB3PGE
Mathew L Parsons
5913 White Rd
Laurel DE 19956

Call Sign: KB3HVD
David A Peterson Jr
28327 Woods Ln
Laurel DE 19956

Call Sign: AC3W
Anderson W Gowens
Laurel DE 19956

FCC Amateur Radio License in Lewes

Call Sign: WA4ZQC
Ronald G Rosin
404 Angola By The Bay
Lewes DE 19958

Call Sign: W3YAH
Elmer R Boyer
Box E132C
Lewes DE 19958

Call Sign: N3ZNY
William E Billings
12 Bradford Ln
Lewes DE 19958

Call Sign: NO3S
Thomas L Fluharty
23854 Brant Cir

Lewes DE 199585388

Call Sign: W3SMA
Paul L Ives Jr
8 Breakwater St
Lewes DE 19958

Call Sign: KB3JPL
Gloria J Horvath
23203 Bridge Way Dr W
Lewes DE 19958

Call Sign: KB3DGJ
Sandor Horvath
23203 Bridgeway Dr W
Lewes DE 19958

Call Sign: KB3JBT
Dustin P Stroup
22361 Camp Arrowhead
Rd
Lewes DE 19958

Call Sign: KB3IHV
David A Hansen
103 Canary Dr
Lewes DE 19958

Call Sign: N3ROJ
Maxime Moise
34381 Carpenters Way
Lewes DE 19958

Call Sign: KB3SPX
Louis F Hopkins
39 Cedarwood Dr
Lewes DE 19958

Call Sign: KB3NXC
Anthony M Zeccola
33542 Creekside Dr
Lewes DE 19958

Call Sign: KB3PGH
Richard L Olson

8 Dartmouth Dr
Lewes DE 19958

Call Sign: W3RLO
Richard L Olson
8 Dartmouth Dr
Lewes DE 19958

Call Sign: W2VSV
Francis J Guyer
15 Dartmouth Dr
Lewes DE 19958

Call Sign: KB3AAA
Anthony F Segreto
34646 Doe Run
Lewes DE 19958

Call Sign: WB3GNO
Raymond E Deskins Jr
22907 Dogwood Dr
Lewes DE 199585222

Call Sign: N3EVG
Bill M Heronemus
113 E 3rd St
Lewes DE 19958

Call Sign: W8QQH
Kenneth J Patterson
119 E Quail Trl
Lewes DE 199581636

Call Sign: KB3MAX
James W Bishop Dds
31259 Edgewood Dr
Lewes DE 19958

Call Sign: KB3IPK
Gale G White
39 Gainsborough Dr
Lewes DE 19958

Call Sign: KB3IPL
James L White

39 Gainsborough Dr
Lewes DE 19958

Call Sign: KB3WBD
James A Harbuck
17319 Graceland Dr
Lewes DE 19958

Call Sign: N3JDK
Ned B Martin
34 Harborview Rd
Lewes DE 19958

Call Sign: K3CFL
Ralph W Curtis Sr
43 Harborview Rd
Lewes DE 19958

Call Sign: KB3CZN
Karen J Brown
31553 Hazzard Dr
Lewes DE 19958

Call Sign: N3PCP
Charles E Clendaniel
31553 Hazzard Dr
Lewes DE 19958

Call Sign: WB2ERL
Robert Henry
33598 Herring View Dr
Lewes DE 19958

Call Sign: W3QJ
Robert Henry
33598 Herring View Dr
Lewes DE 19958

Call Sign: KD3RU
Walt Lupish
1508 Hwy One
Lewes DE 19958

Call Sign: NZ3A
Sarah E Dillon

1508 Hwy One
Lewes DE 19958

Call Sign: W3QHN
Earl H Simmons
31660 Janice Rd C23
Lewes DE 19958

Call Sign: N3KRW
Irvin A Coursey
32430 Lewes Geo Hwy
Lewes DE 19958

Call Sign: KB3EZH
Ronald G Rosin
22934 Linden Dr
Lewes DE 19958

Call Sign: N3UFB
Stanley W Wills
133 Madison Ave
Lewes DE 19958

Call Sign: KB3HTP
Robert A Belknap
108 Maple
Lewes DE 19958

Call Sign: KF3D
Sandra L Horvai Kernosh
17640 Mary Ann Dr
Lewes DE 19958

Call Sign: KC3QD
Amos N Nicholson Sr
31129 Mills Chase Dr
Lewes DE 19958

Call Sign: KA3LIU
James E Vandegrift Jr
17040 Minos Conaway Rd
Lewes DE 199583808

Call Sign: K3RMM
Rita M Mc Clanahan

17437 Minos Conaway Rd
Lewes DE 19958

Call Sign: W3RMM
Robert M Mc Clanahan
17437 Minos Conaway Rd
Lewes DE 19958

Call Sign: KB3HRE
Susan L Halpin
313 Mulberry St
Lewes DE 199581321

Call Sign: WA3PWT
Ronel W Carter
Nassau Park
Lewes DE 19958

Call Sign: KB3MIP
Overfalls Lightship
Amateur Radio Club
120 New Rd
Lewes DE 19958

Call Sign: N1LVI
Bruce S Aldred
120 New Rd
Lewes DE 19958

Call Sign: W3GNQ
Richard N Drevo
15736 New Rd
Lewes DE 19958

Call Sign: WB2JMK
John W Donaway
11 Nottingham Dr Sussex
E
Lewes DE 19958

Call Sign: W3PWT
Ronel W Carter
31603 Oak Ct Wispering
Pines
Lewes DE 19958

Call Sign: K3BAT
Herbert C Morgan Jr
16467 Old Mill Rd
Lewes DE 19958

Call Sign: W3FEG
Edward R Hill
34645 Old Postal Ln
Lewes DE 19958

Call Sign: K3NNZ
Lothar H Meyhofer
13 Pine Water Dr
Lewes DE 199589697

Call Sign: KB3MJS
Madeline S Mccann
31324 Point Cir
Lewes DE 19958

Call Sign: N3GCB
Rita M Mc Clanahan
67 Red Mill Farms
Lewes DE 19958

Call Sign: N4IQU
Timothy J Mc Clanahan
67 Red Mill Farms
Lewes DE 19958

Call Sign: WG4Y
Robert M Mc Clanahan
67 Red Mill Farms
Lewes DE 19958

Call Sign: W3BAY
Timothy J Mc Clanahan
67 Red Mill Farms
Lewes DE 19958

Call Sign: N3SUT
Daniel Ciabattoni Jr
34553 Redfearn Cir
Lewes DE 199589226

Call Sign: N3SXQ
Angeline M Ciabattoni
34553 Redfearn Cir
Lewes DE 199589226

Call Sign: N3LBT
David K Edwards
18179 Robinsonville Rd
Lewes DE 199584403

Call Sign: W3HTV
Russell G Allen
19 Sandpiper Dr
Lewes DE 19958

Call Sign: WB2GMR
Thomas J Negran
32941 Sandstone Dr
Lewes DE 19958

Call Sign: KB3PGC
Anthony S Rousak IV
309301 Sandy Ridge Dr
Lewes DE 19958

Call Sign: N3OLY
Walter J Palmer
66 Sassafras Dr
Lewes DE 19958

Call Sign: N3XPN
Teresa D Giambrone
222 Sassafras Dr
Lewes DE 19958

Call Sign: W4ALT
Walter J Palmer
30735 Sassafras Dr
Lewes DE 19958

Call Sign: W3SWC
Raymond W Riniker
212 Savannah Rd
Lewes DE 19958

Call Sign: WA3TLL
Arthur Tormet
301 Savannah Rd
Lewes DE 19958

Call Sign: KB3IOG
James C Ippolito
609 Savannah Rd
Lewes DE 19958

Call Sign: N2ZBK
Gerard F Cassese
1501 Savannah Rd
Lewes DE 19958

Call Sign: KB3MVF
Joseph H Stormer
430 Seagull Dr
Lewes DE 19958

Call Sign: AB3DK
Joseph H Stormer
430 Seagull Dr
Lewes DE 19958

Call Sign: W3TL
Joseph H Stormer
430 Seagull Dr
Lewes DE 19958

Call Sign: W3AUS
Gerald J Furman
17436 Slipper Shell Way
Unit 8
Lewes DE 19958

Call Sign: K3HLF
Helen L Furman
17436 Slipper Shell Way
Unit 8
Lewes DE 19958

Call Sign: KB3HSY
Bennett J Galvacky

34700 Stardust Dr
Lewes DE 19958

Call Sign: KB3PGI
Stephen Galvacky
34700 Stardust Dr
Mulberry Knoll
Lewes DE 19958

Call Sign: KB3MJL
James J Symons
34341 Summerlyn Dr -
Unit 312
Lewes DE 19958

Call Sign: KA3WWX
Geraldine F Gaines
105 Sweetbriar
Lewes DE 19958

Call Sign: N3IJI
William D Gaines
Sweetbrier
Lewes DE 19958

Call Sign: WB3HEV
Paul G Fair
19741 Tobys Run
Lewes DE 19958

Call Sign: KB3KKO
Leroy A Davis
12 Vermont Ave
Lewes DE 19958

Call Sign: K7DH
Paul G Kratt
410 W 4th St
Lewes DE 199581297

Call Sign: K2GHY
Robert L Lippman
33190 W Batten St
Lewes DE 19958

Call Sign: KB3HSW
Ryan A Palmer
130 W Fourth St
Lewes DE 19958

Call Sign: KG4QWB
Matthew B Simmerman
418 W Fourth St
Lewes DE 19958

Call Sign: KB3MEJ
David Sopa
Westcoats Rd
Lewes DE 19958

Call Sign: N3RSE
Anthony J Monti Jr
320 Woodland Av
Lewes DE 19958

Call Sign: N3WPY
Arlene A Monti
320 Woodland Av
Lewes DE 19958

Call Sign: KA3JFY
Virginia A Doebling
Lewes DE 19958

Call Sign: KB3LAW
Lewes Amateur Radio
Society
Lewes DE 19958

Call Sign: W3LRS
Lewes Amateur Radio
Society
Lewes DE 19958

Call Sign: KA3LMN
Elaine M Burnett
Lewes DE 19958

**FCC Amateur Radio
License in Lincoln**

Call Sign: N3HFF
Vicki N Seabrease
Box 230
Lincoln DE 19960

Call Sign: WB2GLP
Ronald P Davies
Box 438C Rd 1
Lincoln DE 19960

Call Sign: KB3GVN
Don C Macklin
8747 Cedar Creek Rd
Lincoln DE 19960

Call Sign: WA3VUZ
Garry L Davis
Cubbage Pond Rd
Lincoln DE 19960

Call Sign: KB3JBR
Joseph R Buck
18580 Fireside Ln
Lincoln DE 19960

Call Sign: KB3OLF
Frederick J Westwood
16943 Fitzgerald Rd
Lincoln DE 19960

Call Sign: KB3HVG
Melissa A Schutte
10891 Fleatown Rd
Lincoln DE 19960

Call Sign: KB3CGK
Derek H Callaway
2 Hickory Ln
Lincoln DE 19960

Call Sign: WA2WEP
Henry G De Esposito
20005 Johnson Rd
Lincoln DE 19960

Call Sign: WB2WFK
Mary E De Esposito
20005 Johnson Rd
Lincoln DE 19960

Call Sign: N3MZG
Gene E Stover
12029 N Union Church Rd
Lincoln DE 19960

Call Sign: WA3GS
Gene E Stover
12029 N Union Church Rd
Lincoln DE 19960

Call Sign: KB3UVA
Zachary S Keyek
22405 Pinecone Dr
Lincoln DE 19960

Call Sign: W3WRL
William R Leager
22305 Raven Cir
Lincoln DE 19960

Call Sign: N3FFK
Wilton M Neville Sr
5 Ross Rd
Lincoln DE 19960

Call Sign: KB3PGB
Fallon A Mcdonald
21076 W Mayhew Dr
Lincoln DE 19960

Call Sign: KB3SDL
Montana T Mcdonald
21076 W Mayhew Dr
Lincoln DE 19960

Call Sign: KB3HTK
Michael L Stamat
10284 Webb Farm Rd
Lincoln DE 19960

Call Sign: N2QGD
Bryan Doyle
10598 Yellowwood Rd
Lincoln DE 19960

FCC Amateur Radio License in Long Neck

Call Sign: N9VYO
Roger L Level
Breakers Pn Bayside
Long Neck DE 19966

Call Sign: W3GRL
Paul E Widenor
69 Driftwood Dr
Long Neck DE 19966

Call Sign: N3QJM
Julian M Siomkajlo
1547 Morningside Dr
Long Neck DE 19966

Call Sign: KB3HFK
Charlotte I Anderson
304 Teal Rd White House
Beach
Long Neck DE 19966

Call Sign: N3IBE
William B Anderson Sr
304 Teal Rd White House
Beach
Long Neck DE 19966

FCC Amateur Radio License in Magnolia

Call Sign: KB3NRS
Curtis A Kozielec Jr
168 Apple Cross Ln
Magnolia DE 19962

Call Sign: N3AKC

John A Young
Box 24
Magnolia DE 19962

Call Sign: N3PHD
Holland P Woodall Jr
Box 59A
Magnolia DE 19962

Call Sign: AF3R
James O Sevast
48 Cedarfield Rd
Magnolia DE 19962

Call Sign: KA3LNK
Terryl D Sevast
48 Cedarfield Rd
Magnolia DE 19962

Call Sign: N2IMB
Ronald Morella
76 Church Creek Dr
Magnolia DE 19962

Call Sign: N3WAS
Tim F Wade
141 Daffodil Dr
Magnolia DE 19962

Call Sign: KA3KBQ
Jesse D Austin
298 Dogwood Dr
Magnolia DE 19962

Call Sign: KL0NO
Jeffrey B Heller
837 E Pebworth Rd
Magnolia DE 19962

Call Sign: K3JBH
Jeffrey B Heller
837 E Pebworth Rd
Magnolia DE 19962

Call Sign: KB3OIA

Daniel R Evins
53 Marshview Dr
Magnolia DE 19962

Call Sign: N3QQR
Antonio E Browning
56 Marshview Dr
Magnolia DE 19962

Call Sign: KB3VKB
Yenhou C Ng
602 Olde Field Dr
Magnolia DE 19962

Call Sign: N3KWW
Henry Rosario
312 Plaindealing Rd
Magnolia DE 19962

Call Sign: WA2JYZ
Richard H Malone
92 Red Fox Ct
Magnolia DE 19962

Call Sign: N3EOV
James E Ruper
388 Sedgewick Dr
Magnolia DE 19962

Call Sign: N3TMJ
Timothy E Murray
254 Sophers Row
Magnolia DE 199629304

Call Sign: K3MU
Timothy E Murray
254 Sophers Row
Magnolia DE 199629304

Call Sign: KB3FLB
Russell A Morris
140 Stevenson Dr
Magnolia DE 19962

Call Sign: K3JCT

John C Tillinghast Sr
651 Tullamore Ct
Magnolia DE 19962

Call Sign: N3NGU
Frank E Deo
662 Tullamore Ct
Magnolia DE 19962

Call Sign: N3YUK
Donn R Jarrell
Magnolia DE 19962

FCC Amateur Radio License in Marshalton

Call Sign: KA3ILO
Willard R Semple
2816 Newport Gap Pike
Marshallton DE 19808

Call Sign: KB3OKC
Willard R Semple
2816 Newport Gap Pike
Marshallton DE 19808

FCC Amateur Radio License in Marydel

Call Sign: W3HLB
James W Remondi
Box 256A Rd 1
Marydel DE 19964

Call Sign: N3NGR
Edward H Riemer
Box 269
Marydel DE 19964

Call Sign: KB3EVG
Timothy R Christ
3716 Mahan Corner Rd
Marydel DE 19964

Call Sign: KB0LYC

Edward C Heddinger Jr
439 Tappahannak Trl
Marydel DE 19964

Call Sign: KB3TJY
James E Schimmelman
2972 Westville Rd
Marydel DE 19964

Call Sign: WA3ZFY
Hollis T Christian Jr
Marydel DE 19964

FCC Amateur Radio License in Middletown

Call Sign: KB3FCI
Wayne E Boulden
231 Acorn Dr
Middletown DE 19709

Call Sign: N3EDK
James C Stewart
113 Airmont Dr
Middletown DE 19709

Call Sign: WB3DLU
Robert L Vawter
1121 Bayview Rd
Middletown DE 19709

Call Sign: WB2TLE
Henry B Greever Jr
1137 Bayview Rd
Middletown DE 19709

Call Sign: KB3VLB
Martin E Keefe
333 Beech Ln
Middletown DE 19709

Call Sign: AA3A
Martin E Keefe
333 Beech Ln
Middletown DE 19709

Call Sign: KB3OXM
Ruth E Kliment
1441 Bunker Hill Rd
Middletown DE 19709

Call Sign: KB3PTK
Gavin K Connolly
331 Clayton Manor Dr
Middletown DE 19709

Call Sign: KB3JAO
Laura A Jordan
18 Crenshaw Ct
Middletown DE 19709

Call Sign: KB3CIQ
Vaughn A Le Sage
205 Deerfield Dr
Middletown DE 19709

Call Sign: WA3X
Paul M Matarese
1160 Dutchneck Rd
Middletown DE 19709

Call Sign: N3CHQ
Paul J Knight
112 E Delaware Canal Ct
Middletown DE 19709

Call Sign: N3PJK
Paul J Knight
112 E Delaware Canal Ct
Middletown DE 19709

Call Sign: W3EDB
Robert W Donovan
115 E Green St
Middletown DE 19709

Call Sign: KB1EBC
Robert C Mac Donald
311 E Harvest Ln

Middletown DE
197093039

Call Sign: W3WU
George W Daly
6 E Minglewood Dr
Middletown DE 19709

Call Sign: KA2PMP
George Buchanan
214 E Union Dr
Middletown DE 19709

Call Sign: N3MWQ
Walter T Gale III
204 E Wayne Way
Middletown DE
197093812

Call Sign: KC7WEK
Drexel T Evans Jr
312 Elizabeth St
Middletown DE 19709

Call Sign: W3LES
Leslie R Britton Jr
107 Fairfield Ct
Middletown DE 19709

Call Sign: W3XHF
Leslie R Britton Jr
107 Fairfield Ct
Middletown DE 19709

Call Sign: NQ3H
Leslie R Britton Jr
107 Fairfield Ct
Middletown DE 19709

Call Sign: KB3OJM
James R Oborne Jr
4 Fredricksburg Dr
Middletown DE 19709

Call Sign: W3YE

James R Oborne Jr
4 Fredricksburg Dr
Middletown DE 19709

Call Sign: KB3PMW
Jeffrey M Stobart
6 Harding Ct
Middletown DE 19709

Call Sign: KB3LLF
Delaware Valley County
Hunters Assoc
803 Holly Ct
Middletown DE
197099309

Call Sign: AG3X
Delaware Valley County
Hunters Assoc
803 Holly Ct
Middletown DE
197099309

Call Sign: KD4UTI
Rodney V Smith
803 Holly Ct
Middletown DE
197099309

Call Sign: N3FC
Rodney V Smith
803 Holly Ct
Middletown DE
197099309

Call Sign: KB3PZM
Kathleen A Conrade
204 Horseshoe Dr
Middletown DE 19709

Call Sign: N3MIC
Gene W Cole Jr
331 Hostetter Blvd
Middletown DE 19709

Call Sign: KB3GRV
Mark W Rinehart
311 John Randal Dr
Middletown DE 19709

Call Sign: N3ZJW
Robert G Vormwald
527 Lake Dr
Middletown DE 19709

Call Sign: KF6MMP
Gregory A Baize
113 Lakeside Dr
Middletown DE
197091374

Call Sign: N3LOB
Michael H Abernathy Sr
134 Laks Dr
Middletown DE 19709

Call Sign: N3MMI
Ernesto L Perez Sr
109 Leanne Dr
Middletown DE
197099101

Call Sign: N3NHD
Leslie R Britton Jr
559 Maple Ave
Middletown DE 19709

Call Sign: KB3IBN
John A Lucey
130 Marathon Dr
Middletown DE 19709

Call Sign: KB3IHQ
Clarence A Brooks
33 Millwood Dr
Middletown DE 19709

Call Sign: WA3ZAV
Geoffrey H Fallows
104 Peachtree Ln

Middletown DE 19709

Call Sign: WB3DHX
Earl L Emerson Jr
100 Phillips Dr Box 232
Middletown DE 19709

Call Sign: N3UCJ
Oliver A Manalo
142 Pine Valley
Middletown DE 19709

Call Sign: KD3DH
James F White Sr
107 Pine Valley Dr
Middletown DE 19709

Call Sign: KB3BXO
Glenn A Louk
604 Pleasant Ln
Middletown DE 19709

Call Sign: K3UIN
Ronald E Andrzejewski
631 Poets Way
Middletown DE 19709

Call Sign: KA3CDB
Herbert L Groh
554 Port Penn Rd
Middletown DE 19709

Call Sign: WB3DHY
James L Chester
805 S Scott St
Middletown DE 19709

Call Sign: KB3YDV
Richard A Baggs
27 Springmill Dr
Middletown DE 19709

Call Sign: KB3JAR
Ray R Schinzel
105 St Augustine Ct

Middletown DE 19709

Call Sign: KA3BOF
Jo A Schuyler
271 Sugar Pine Dr
Middletown DE 19709

Call Sign: WB3DDS
Thomas L Schuyler
271 Sugar Pine Dr
Middletown DE 19709

Call Sign: KB3RBZ
Stephen V Serencko
377 Thomas Landing Rd
Middletown DE 19709

Call Sign: K3MOT
Stephen V Serencko
377 Thomas Landing Rd
Middletown DE 19709

Call Sign: KD3J
Neil S Jarrett Jr
417 W Harvest Ln
Middletown DE 19709

Call Sign: KB3VLU
Brian D Driscall
8 W Minglewood Dr
Middletown DE 19709

Call Sign: K3BDD
Brian D Driscall
8 W Minglewood Dr
Middletown DE 19709

Call Sign: KA3RER
Alfonso E Dalton
48 W Minglewood Dr
Middletown DE 19709

Call Sign: KA3WQD
Robert P Bridwell Jr
169 Wellington Way

Middletown DE 19709

Call Sign: KB3GQT
Diane C Gillespie
Middletown DE 19709

**FCC Amateur Radio
License in Milford**

Call Sign: WD8PXM
Roy K Holsather
511 Ashley Way
Milford DE 19963

Call Sign: K3ABL
Roy K Holsather
511 Ashley Way
Milford DE 19963

Call Sign: WA2VQV
Russell W Young Jr
153 Aspen Ct
Milford DE 19963

Call Sign: K3AOT
John R Winward
184 Bowman Rd
Milford DE 199635362

Call Sign: N4ETK
Ralph L Vasa
Box 213D
Milford DE 19963

Call Sign: N3BFK
Frank A Newton
Box 325
Milford DE 19963

Call Sign: N3EFR
Robert E L Purvis
Box 332
Milford DE 19963

Call Sign: WB3GWE

Clarence C Biddle Jr
Box 508
Milford DE 19963

Call Sign: W3FBI
Gary E Emeigh
1294 Canterbury Rd
Milford DE 19963

Call Sign: KE2AU
John H Wallace
899 Church Hill Rd
Milford DE 199635544

Call Sign: N3OMV
William L Vincent
1401 Church Hill Rd
Milford DE 19963

Call Sign: K1YGF
David L Richards
18 Clearview Dr
Milford DE 19963

Call Sign: W8AZZ
Gilbert A Fishbeck
100 Delaware Veterans Dr
Milford DE 19963

Call Sign: KB3JUQ
Kyle R Moore
6 Dot St
Milford DE 19963

Call Sign: N3NXR
Ross B Hicks
9090 Draper Rd
Milford DE 19963

Call Sign: KB3NXR
Ross B Hicks
9090 Drapper Rd
Milford DE 19963

Call Sign: W3RZD

Robert C Green
11 E Yorktown Rd
Milford DE 19963

Call Sign: KA3ROL
Matthew S Karol
20055 Elks Lodge Rd
Milford DE 19963

Call Sign: WA3S
Warren C Phillips Jr
414 Evergreen Cir
Milford DE 19963

Call Sign: KB3OKI
Granville E Hastings
312 Fisher Ave
Milford DE 19963

Call Sign: W3TRY
Granville Terry E Hastings
Jr
312 Fisher Ave
Milford DE 19963

Call Sign: KB3NKA
Matthew S Karol
316 Hall Pl
Milford DE 19963

Call Sign: K3RM
Roland H Metzner
359 Jenkins Pond Rd
Milford DE 19963

Call Sign: KB3MJT
Justin B Hopkins
434 Kings Highway
Milford DE 19963

Call Sign: N3ILX
William J Dodenhoff
874 Log Cabin Rd
Milford DE 19963

Call Sign: W3PVO
George S Williams
6709 Marshall St
Milford DE 199632412

Call Sign: K3FSP
Lewis H Dickerson
500 Marvel Rd
Milford DE 19963

Call Sign: KB3CGL
William A Hardy
604 Mccolley St
Milford DE 199632312

Call Sign: KB3SHM
Frederick R Stocker
17 Mccoy St
Milford DE 19963

Call Sign: K3RUF
Bernard Frankel
704 Meadow Brook Ln
Milford DE 19963

Call Sign: W3MAW
David S Hagen
686 N Dupont Hwy
Milford DE 19963

Call Sign: KB3HEW
David S Hagen
686 N Dupont Hwy
Milford DE 19963

Call Sign: K3NII
William G Wiest
135 N Landing Dr
Milford DE 19963

Call Sign: KB3JGE
Allen S Jester Jr
401 N Rehobeth Blvd
Milford DE 19963

Call Sign: W3JWH
William Gray Jr
215 N Rehoboth Blvd
Milford DE 19963

Call Sign: WA3RJZ
Nelson R Gray Sr
215 N Rehoboth Blvd
Milford DE 19963

Call Sign: K3ABX
Nelson R Gray Sr
N Rehoboth Blvd
Milford DE 19963

Call Sign: KA3WYC
Michael D Herholdt
8406 N Union Church Rd
Milford DE 19963

Call Sign: KD3UJ
Elmer R Boyer Jr
701 N Washington St
Milford DE 19963

Call Sign: W3YAH
Elmer R Boyer Jr
701 N Washington St
Milford DE 19963

Call Sign: KC3XQ
Richard C Webb
6127 Old Shawnee Rd
Milford DE 19963

Call Sign: KA3DDB
Christopher L Carter
6331 Old Shawnee Rd
Milford DE 19963

Call Sign: WB3FEF
Joseph T Cassey III
5850 Old Shawnee Rd
Milford DE 19963

Call Sign: W3UWO
Christopher L Carter
6331 Old Shawnee Rd
Milford DE 19963

Call Sign: WA3WZV
Howard J Moore
12 Pennsylvania Ave
Milford DE 19963

Call Sign: W3ZAC
Walter O Sutton Jr
292 Purple Finch Ln
Milford DE 19963

Call Sign: W3BKN
Wilbur T Haight
314 S Du Pont Blvd
Milford DE 19963

Call Sign: AI3G
William D Ermer
S Sagamore Dr
Milford DE 19963

Call Sign: KB3PMN
Joseph C Zimmerman Jr
306 S Washington St
Milford DE 19963

Call Sign: KC4OGB
Manuel Rodriguez Diaz
422 S Washington St
Milford DE 19963

Call Sign: W3VQA
Gilbert D Murphy
404 S Washington St
Milford DE 19963

Call Sign: KC2HKT
Michael S Moran
30068 Stage Coach Cir
Milford DE 19963

Call Sign: N3RKS
Robert Smith
109 Thompsonville Rd
Milford DE 19963

Call Sign: KB3DYG
Pamela A Benton
714 Tub Mill Pond Rd
Milford DE 19963

Call Sign: KB3VST
Thomas B Daniels
3680 Tub Mill Pond Rd
Milford DE 19963

Call Sign: KA3MMJ
Joseph E James Sr
8 W Clarke Ave
Milford DE 19963

Call Sign: KA3OUH
Joseph A Mullaney II
1 W Thrush Dr
Milford DE 19963

Call Sign: KF4WLE
George A Babel
6140 Williamsville Rd
Milford DE 19963

Call Sign: W3UWO
Willis L Carter
611 Woodmere Rd
Milford DE 19963

Call Sign: N3LGO
Carlisle W Hall Jr
7 Woodside Dr
Milford DE 19963

Call Sign: WB3BXM
Earle E Worthington
Milford DE 19963

Call Sign: W3YFI

Oscar D Bailey
Milford DE 19963

FCC Amateur Radio License in Millsboro

Call Sign: W3IAU
Walter J Staniszewski Jr
8th St
Millsboro DE 19966

Call Sign: W3FIP
Frank I Pannebaker Jr
25844 American Ave
Millsboro DE 19966

Call Sign: W3KAP
Kathleen A Pannebaker
25844 American Ave
Millsboro DE 19966

Call Sign: K3RBP
William J Stief Jr
7 Bay Point Rd
Millsboro DE 19966

Call Sign: WA3WTO
Reidun Stief
7 Bay Point Rd
Millsboro DE 19966

Call Sign: W3LF
Randy K Murray
24656 Betts Pond Rd
Millsboro DE 19966

Call Sign: WB9PXN
John L Turner
34189 Black Pine Ln
Millsboro DE 19966

Call Sign: N3UMX
William D Danner
196 Bobbys Branch Rd
Millsboro DE 19966

Call Sign: N3UFF
Jayne D Battersby
Box 171
Millsboro DE 199669525

Call Sign: N3WEO
Joseph L Vaughan
Box 173 B1
Millsboro DE 19966

Call Sign: N3UFC
Todd O Cropper
Box 500
Millsboro DE 19966

Call Sign: KA3SYZ
Jonas C Walker Jr
Box 518A
Millsboro DE 19966

Call Sign: AA3RT
Wayne S Bowden
Box 894
Millsboro DE 19966

Call Sign: WI3P
Thomas Collins Jr
5101 Caitlin's Way
Millsboro DE 199663735

Call Sign: KA1MOR
James W Mac Farland
26982 Canvasback Rd Pot
Nets Bayside
Millsboro DE 19966

Call Sign: N3CJE
John H Howell Jr
19 Captains Way Bx A9
Millsboro DE 19966

Call Sign: KB3UUZ
Bryce P Wharton
20512 Careys Camp Rd

Millsboro DE 19966

Call Sign: KB3MEB
Martin L Kirby
22255 Careys Camp Rd
Millsboro DE 19966

Call Sign: W3MLK
Martin L Kirby
22255 Careys Camp Rd
Millsboro DE 19966

Call Sign: N3JVT
Justin V Timmons
22255 Carey's Camp Rd
Millsboro DE 19966

Call Sign: KB3MFG
Justin V Timmons
22255 Carey's Cp Rd
Millsboro DE 19966

Call Sign: W1GZE
Paul W Kercher I
24112 Cari Dr
Millsboro DE 19966

Call Sign: WB3HPP
James F Mc Lear Jr
26778 Castaway Cir
Millsboro DE 199665977

Call Sign: KA3HUN
Edward G Serman Jr
334 Church St
Millsboro DE 19966

Call Sign: KB3UVL
Nicholas C Pippin
51 Comanche Cir
Millsboro DE 19966

Call Sign: KB3MOO
Donald J Smith
23128 Country Living Rd

Millsboro DE 19966

Call Sign: KB3OHX
Hayden J Smith
23128 Country Living Rd
Millsboro DE 19966

Call Sign: KB3QJ
Frederick D Herrmann Sr
26206 Cove Dr Mc
Millsboro DE 19966

Call Sign: KA3DYX
Robert B Taney
63 Creek Dr
Millsboro DE 19966

Call Sign: KC2MEV
Anthony L Esposito
34441 Fleet St
Millsboro DE 19966

Call Sign: KB3MQU
Jacob A Lester
23581 Godwin School Rd
Millsboro DE 19966

Call Sign: KB3MBL
William J Prettyman
23581 Godwin School Rd
Millsboro DE 19966

Call Sign: W3HRT
William J Prettyman
23581 Godwin School Rd
Millsboro DE 19966

Call Sign: W3DR
William J Prettyman
23581 Godwin School Rd
Millsboro DE 19966

Call Sign: KB3NZJ
Jerry D Martin Jr
25399 Guinea Hollow Rd

Millsboro DE 19966

Call Sign: KB3TCH
Paula J Martin
25399 Guinea Hollow Rd
Millsboro DE 19966

Call Sign: N3QQS
Sheila M Bowden
28324 Harmony Cemetery
Rd
Millsboro DE 19966

Call Sign: KB3GNN
Wayne S Bowden
28324 Harmony Cemetery
Rd
Millsboro DE 19966

Call Sign: KB3GSY
Sean R Bowden
28324 Harmony Cemetery
Rd
Millsboro DE 19966

Call Sign: KB3LFS
Andrew T Johnson
196 Jersey Rd
Millsboro DE 19966

Call Sign: KB3ISA
Wilson R Merchant
25942 Kings Ln
Enchanted Acres
Millsboro DE 19966

Call Sign: KE3QR
Charles W Klaus
33425 Lakeshore Cir
Millsboro DE 199665940

Call Sign: KB3JUR
Jon D Monroe
47 Lakeview Dr
Millsboro DE 19966

Call Sign: KB3LAR
Charles W Headley
29658 Lewis Rd
Millsboro DE 19966

Call Sign: KB3OKV
Brandon D Snyder
67 Oak Dr
Millsboro DE 19966

Call Sign: AA4MX
Ralph L Mc Donald
Rehoboth Shores
Millsboro DE 19966

Call Sign: N3KQ
Charles W Headley
29658 Lewis Rd
Millsboro DE 19966

Call Sign: KB3QIH
Mike A Merchant
32681 Oak Orchard Rd
Millsboro DE 19966

Call Sign: KB3SDG
Tyler Edge
31378 River Rd
Millsboro DE 19966

Call Sign: W3CJO
John R Dick Jr
29803 Lewis Rd
Millsboro DE 19966

Call Sign: W3IOU
Wilson R Merchant
32681 Oak Orchard Rd
Millsboro DE 19966

Call Sign: N3HXS
Edward L Porter
24280 Rivers Edge Rd
Millsboro DE 19966

Call Sign: KB3SDJ
Jay C Jolly
20149 Lowes Crossing
Millsboro DE 19966

Call Sign: KB3DUQ
Charles J Wilkerson
36304 Pear Tree Rd
Millsboro DE 19966

Call Sign: N3BZG
Frank A Hopkins
Rt 302 305 & 48
Millsboro DE 19966

Call Sign: WA3QVJ
Benjamin J Harte Jr
18975 Lowes Rd
Millsboro DE 19966

Call Sign: KB3CJA
Robert W Wilkerson
36338 Pear Tree Rd
Millsboro DE 19966

Call Sign: KB3WIL
Leonard Ballas
23718 Samuel Adams Cir
Millsboro DE 19966

Call Sign: KB3WZE
William D Robinson
30844 Magenta Ln
Millsboro DE 19966

Call Sign: KB3JPM
William R Sammons
97 Pine Dr
Millsboro DE 19966

Call Sign: K3PIP
Leonard Ballas
23718 Samuel Adams Cir
Millsboro DE 19966

Call Sign: KB3UVB
Lacy Perdue
22994 Mission Rd
Millsboro DE 19966

Call Sign: W3WTE
Glenn A Laser
23105 Pine Run
Millsboro DE 19966

Call Sign: K2NEW
Nathan E Wise
23730 Samuel Adams Cir
Millsboro DE 19966

Call Sign: N3ELK
Keith R Timmons
25605 Morris Mill Rd
Millsboro DE 19966

Call Sign: KB3VOQ
James W Crew
294 Pond Rd
Millsboro DE 19966

Call Sign: KB3PGK
John M Dill
25863 Sandpiper Ct
Millsboro DE 19966

Call Sign: N3IBB
John L Pachuta Sr
18 Nob Hill N
Millsboro DE 19966

Call Sign: WA3SLT
Edward F Price
314 Pond Rd
Millsboro DE 19966

Call Sign: KB2RS
George R Gordon
133 Sandridge Ct
Millsboro DE 19966

Call Sign: W6SHA
John L Ballantyne
32729 Spring Water Dr
Millsboro DE 19966

Call Sign: KC3TG
Joseph W Cain Jr
26686 Starboard Rd
Millsboro DE 19966

Call Sign: N3IIU
Sharon M Anderson
Tucks Rd Lot 8
Millsboro DE 19966

Call Sign: N3AVU
Albert C Gibson
34063 Village Way
Millsboro DE 19966

Call Sign: WA3CDV
Thomas J Sullivan Jr
5 Ward Way
Millsboro DE 19966

Call Sign: N3JCE
Meran Gosthnian
122 William Dr
Millsboro DE 19966

Call Sign: KB3TXU
Samuel J Schiffer
27119 Windjammer Rd
Millsboro DE 19966

Call Sign: W7IKM
Robert J Mc Mahon
Millsboro DE 19966

Call Sign: N3YYW
Rachel S Hudson
Millsboro DE 19966

Call Sign: N3ZFM

George W Hudson
Millsboro DE 19966

Call Sign: KB3MQV
Calvin L Abbott
Millsboro DE 19966

Call Sign: KB3OLM
Christopher A Mitchell
Millsboro DE 19966

Call Sign: KB3JUM
Scott W Van Der Wall
Millsboro DE 19966

FCC Amateur Radio License in Millville

Call Sign: KB3WZF
Robert W Gordon
35235 Atlantic Ave
Millville DE 19967

Call Sign: N3KDH
Gerald N Fournier
Box 31
Millville DE 19970

Call Sign: K3RJG
Ronald J Gillenardo
18 Dockside Dr
Millville DE 19967

Call Sign: WB2AXR
Audry L Barnum
506 Lake Ct
Millville DE 19970

Call Sign: KB3OQK
Amos B Scott
7 Lisa Ave
Millville DE 19970

Call Sign: KB3WZI
Richard T Shoobridge

35023 Tybee St
Millville DE 19967

FCC Amateur Radio License in Milton

Call Sign: WB3HUH
George W Walker Jr
1502 Beach Plum Dr
Milton DE 19968

Call Sign: KA2DJQ
John A Mac Carthy
Box 111Aaa
Milton DE 19968

Call Sign: K3HXG
Charles T Wolstenholme
Box 268
Milton DE 19968

Call Sign: KA3OQE
John J Hill
Box 29
Milton DE 19968

Call Sign: KB3LFR
Roy T Collins
307 Broadkill Rd
Milton DE 19968

Call Sign: N3ALR
Ira R Baker
403 Chestnut St
Milton DE 19968

Call Sign: WV3I
Albert C Freischmidt Jr
12532 Coastal Hwy
Milton DE 19968

Call Sign: KB3SDM
Tighmir I Sayles
215 Coulter St
Milton DE 19968

Call Sign: KB3NRC
Wyatt Spellman
41 Cripple Creek Run
Milton DE 19958

Call Sign: KC2OCC
Joseph J Marino
16778 Gravel Hill Rd
Milton DE 19968

Call Sign: N3YMB
Gene B Mc Natt
17113 Gravel Hill Rd
Milton DE 19968

Call Sign: WB3CHC
John W Poore Jr
16406 Hudson Rd
Milton DE 19968

Call Sign: K3JP
John W Poore Jr
16406 Hudson Rd
Milton DE 19968

Call Sign: KB3UUY
Caleb R Hagan
20 Meadowridge Ln
Milton DE 19968

Call Sign: WA3KOP
Gerald A Blakeslee
117 Morris Ave
Milton DE 199681029

Call Sign: K3GRZ
Gerald A Blakeslee
117 Morris Ave
Milton DE 199681029

Call Sign: WB3LPL
Douglas C Lodge
109 New Mexico Ave
Milton DE 19968

Call Sign: KB3HPR
John K King
109 Pond Dr
Milton DE 19968

Call Sign: W3VQC
John K King
109 Pond Dr
Milton DE 19968

Call Sign: KC2IEY
Michael R Mcnamara
106 Sailor Ln
Milton DE 19968

Call Sign: N3MRM
Michael R Mcnamara
106 Sailor Ln
Milton DE 19968

Call Sign: KB3JBS
Charles F Betyeman
20 Shay Ln
Milton DE 19968

Call Sign: W3DEL
Charles F Betyeman
20 Shay Ln
Milton DE 19968

Call Sign: KB3OMW
Cheek E Robert
25404 Smithway
Milton DE 19968

Call Sign: KB3KYH
William S Duveneck
18682 Sunny Sky Blvd
Milton DE 19968

Call Sign: KB7FPW
William R Kaler
12419 Union St Extended
Milton DE 19968

FCC Amateur Radio License in Montchanin

Call Sign: WB3LBP
Jack W Ballou
Box 142
Montchanin DE 19710

FCC Amateur Radio License in Nassau

Call Sign: KB3GDZ
Bn Amateur Radio Club
Nassau DE 19969

Call Sign: NU3DE
Bn Amateur Radio Club
Nassau DE 19969

Call Sign: KB3GVG
Kevin S Smith
Nassau DE 19969

Call Sign: KB3GVH
Colleen L Smith
Nassau DE 19969

FCC Amateur Radio License in New Castle

Call Sign: KB3MPN
Emmett C Plant
408 Aberdeen Cir
New Castle DE 19720

Call Sign: WB3HYJ
William B Raker Jr
20 Adair Ave
New Castle DE 19720

Call Sign: AC3S
Albert F Harrington
10 Allegretto Rd
New Castle DE 197201504

Call Sign: K3SUY
Eugene S Bell
2 Allegretto Rd Du Ross
Heights
New Castle DE 19720

Call Sign: W3OWE
Bernard J Matyniak Sr
58 Appleby Rd
New Castle DE 19720

Call Sign: N3TBC
David J Knight
19 Auburn Dr
New Castle DE 19720

Call Sign: K3SM
Michael Spinazzola
12 Bancroft Rd
New Castle DE 19720

Call Sign: N3HGR
Raymond J Beckham
16 Bassett Ave
New Castle DE 19720

Call Sign: NI3B
Brian G Pasternak
5 Beacon Ln
New Castle DE 19720

Call Sign: KB3GQS
Carol B Harrington
1106 Bear Rd
New Castle DE 197204604

Call Sign: N3XJR
Emeka O Nwankwo
4 Blyth Ct
New Castle DE 19720

Call Sign: KE3LK
Russell D Stafford Jr
Box 426

New Castle DE 19720

Call Sign: KB3UDR
William L Strupczewski
26 Bradbury Rd
New Castle DE 19720

Call Sign: N3XCS
Julius J Hicks
2 Briar Cliff Dr
New Castle DE 19720

Call Sign: N3BNC
Henry G Dale
117 Buck Ln
New Castle DE 19720

Call Sign: KB3BEG
Jose L Aponte
26 Candlewick Ct
New Castle DE 19720

Call Sign: KB3QCW
Beverly J Wise
1228 Canvasback Dr
New Castle DE 19720

Call Sign: N3UQT
Anthony J Marge
144 Casimir Dr
New Castle DE 19720

Call Sign: KB3OJH
Andrew Bounds
27 Caxton Dr
New Castle DE 19720

Call Sign: KA3KGH
Daniel M Vitalo
38 Cherry Rd
New Castle DE 19720

Call Sign: N3EDO
William P Bouchard
95 Chesterfield Dr

New Castle DE 19720

Call Sign: KA3PKY
Chris E Smith
17 Chiming Rd
New Castle DE 19720

Call Sign: N3ESZ
Lester E Smith Sr
17 Chiming Rd Carriage
Run
New Castle DE 19720

Call Sign: KB3PTN
David G Carpenter Jr
5 Cobblestone Dr Colton
Meadow
New Castle DE 19720

Call Sign: N3QHD
Patrick K Johnston
36 Commonwealth Blvd
New Castle DE 19720

Call Sign: N3ZIH
Jorge L Cabrera Sr
138 Cross Ave
New Castle DE 19720

Call Sign: KC8TJW
Jonathan R Frush
628 Dane Ct
New Castle DE 19720

Call Sign: KB3TSV
Daniel A Nolte III
107 Delaware Ave
New Castle DE 19720

Call Sign: KB3TSU
Brad R Karan
120 Delaware Ave
New Castle DE 19720

Call Sign: WB3JVT

John C Kochur
24 Donwood Dr
New Castle DE 19720

Call Sign: KB3FEH
Thomas P Manchester
22 Dryden Rd
New Castle DE 19720

Call Sign: N3WLC
Stanley P Shipkowski
144 Dutton Ct
New Castle DE 19720

Call Sign: N2USR
Jeffrey M Mc Craney
109 Dyer Ave
New Castle DE 19720

Call Sign: K3EVY
Frederick V Tarburton Jr
110 E 2nd St
New Castle DE 19720

Call Sign: KB3GAH
Calvin B Strachan
22 E 6th St
New Castle DE 197205088

Call Sign: N3PWC
Renee D Pauls
59 E Bellamy Dr
New Castle DE 19720

Call Sign: AE3H
Charles E Sculley
103 E Van Buren Ave
New Castle DE 197203321

Call Sign: KE3CR
Giles W Berry
704 East Ave
New Castle DE 197206219

Call Sign: WA3RED

Ronald W Snyder
134 Edge Ave Swanwyck
Ests
New Castle DE 19720

Call Sign: KB3DGI
Danny P Aument
32 Fairhaven Ct
New Castle DE 19720

Call Sign: K3BBR
William L Preis
2 Finney Rd Penn Acres
New Castle DE 19720

Call Sign: KB2UIT
Rafael C Cruz
25 Gail Rd
New Castle DE 197201709

Call Sign: W3GL
Ralph L Duvall Jr
704 Granthams Ln
New Castle DE 19720

Call Sign: AA3IZ
Farouk N Ahamad
103 Harrison Ave
Wilmington Manor
New Castle DE 19720

Call Sign: N3XJV
Frank J Tampanello
304 Hazlett Ave
New Castle DE 19720

Call Sign: KB3RBK
Charles H Tucker
19 Heddington Rd
New Castle DE 19720

Call Sign: NT3E
Frederick S Sowers
18 Hillview Ave Mayview
Mnr

New Castle DE 19720

Call Sign: N3AYF
I Mae Leamy
10 Holly Dr
New Castle DE 19720

Call Sign: WA3TPD
H Barton Leamy
10 Holly Dr
New Castle DE 19720

Call Sign: KB3FEI
Dale L Matthews
33 Hunter Rd
New Castle DE 19720

Call Sign: N3NZS
Andrew M Winters
29 Hunter Rd
New Castle DE 19720

Call Sign: KA3CMA
Gregory Daniels
205 Jefferson Ave
New Castle DE 19720

Call Sign: KA3YXL
Thomas M Bart
124 Lea Rd
New Castle DE 197201820

Call Sign: K3ESP
Thomas M Bart
124 Lea Rd
New Castle DE 197201820

Call Sign: WB3KVD
Thomas W Pollard
124 Louise Rd
New Castle DE 19720

Call Sign: N3XCP
Pablo Garcia Castaneda
14 Mark Dr

New Castle DE 19720

Call Sign: N3TEE
Shawn H Rullens
43 Marlborough Ct
New Castle DE 19720

Call Sign: KB3VLR
Roy W Brimer
209 Mccallmont Rd
New Castle DE 19720

Call Sign: KB3RVR
Wayne H Hale
409 Moores Ln
New Castle DE 19720

Call Sign: KB3FEG
Dustin M Brown
109 Morrison Rd
New Castle DE 19720

Call Sign: WN3EOC
New Castle County
Emergency Operations
Group
3601 N Dupont Hwy
New Castle DE 19720

Call Sign: KB3NKH
Eric I Arnoth
166 N Katrin Cir
New Castle DE 19720

Call Sign: WA3IWI
Vernon A James
4 Nicole Ct
New Castle DE 19720

Call Sign: WB3ESJ
Walter J Szymanski
10 Oregon Ave
New Castle DE 19720

Call Sign: KB3JUA

Shawn E Jackson
512 Paisley Ln
New Castle DE 19720

Call Sign: KD3JJ
Fabian Spadaccini
438 Pigeon View Ln
New Castle DE 19720

Call Sign: N3AVG
Robert J Morgan Jr
1 Prestwick Ct
New Castle DE 19720

Call Sign: KA3TNF
Mark S Slaymaker
104 Prestwick Dr
New Castle DE 197203023

Call Sign: KB3YGA
Horace L Pedrick Jr
30 Quindome Dr
New Castle DE 19720

Call Sign: KF4JPE
Charles J Mckenna
1 Reads Way Suite 200
New Castle DE 19720

Call Sign: KA3UXR
Grady R Burns Sr
12 Revelle St
New Castle DE 197203933

Call Sign: N3QFD
Chris J Merio
6 Robert Rd
New Castle DE 19720

Call Sign: N3VRU
Sidney W Courtney Jr
10 Robert Rd
New Castle DE 19720

Call Sign: AB8NG

Thomas G O Connor Jr
102 Rodney Dr
New Castle DE 19720

Call Sign: N3QNJ
Mark J Marshall
239 Romeo Dr
New Castle DE 19720

Call Sign: KB3QNO
Joseph James
Kannampuzha
550 S Dupont Hwy Apt 5O
New Castle DE 19720

Call Sign: KA3WOW
Monte L Bellon
30 S Independence Blvd
New Castle DE 19720

Call Sign: K3COV
Nicholas A Di Girolamo Sr
214 Schafer Blvd
New Castle DE 197204724

Call Sign: KA3FPE
Reese I Savage
213 Southerland Dr
New Castle DE 19720

Call Sign: KB3VBB
Richard C Marsh
730 Staghorn Dr
New Castle DE 19702

Call Sign: KB3IBP
Peter V Rogers
451 Stonebridge Blvd
New Castle DE 197206715

Call Sign: KA3LBJ
David C Driscall
124 Stonehurst Ct
New Castle DE 19720

Call Sign: N3TAC
Raymond P Suhocki
122 Stonehurst Ct Ashton
New Castle DE 19720

Call Sign: N3SKI
Eugene S Bell Jr
18 Strawbridge Ave
New Castle DE 19720

Call Sign: WB3KQY
Ronald G Porter
15 Tatlow Ln
New Castle DE 19720

Call Sign: K0ALB
Albert L Berkes
507 Tremont St
New Castle DE 19720

Call Sign: KB3VFL
Paul A Glazewski
17 University Ave
New Castle DE 19720

Call Sign: WF3K
John C Tillinghast Sr
12 Van Dyke Dr
New Castle DE 19720

Call Sign: KA3NLV
Randall C Weaver
15 Varmar Dr
New Castle DE 19720

Call Sign: KB3AWO
Reuben W Mc Vey III
104 W 10th St
New Castle DE 19702

Call Sign: KB3UIJ
Christian L Hackman
616 W 13th St
New Castle DE 19720

Call Sign: KB3JIE
Nicholas A Sowa
308 W Franklin Ave
New Castle DE 19720

Call Sign: KB3IRZ
Craig M Cannon
218 W Grant Ave
New Castle DE 19720

Call Sign: KB3JF
Frank N Howell
206 W Roosevelt Ave
New Castle DE 19720

Call Sign: KD3LU
Mary K Dean
40 Wardor Ave
New Castle DE 19720

Call Sign: KA3SNC
Michael E Kibler
9 Wellesley Ct
New Castle DE 19720

Call Sign: KB3SIB
William C Lyons
907 Wildel Ave
New Castle DE 19720

Call Sign: W3LYT
George L Hawkins
1200 Wilmington Rd
New Castle DE 19720

Call Sign: KB2OXR
Kevin H Mc Call
21 Windmill Ln Apt 20
New Castle DE 19720

Call Sign: KB3JAN
Tyrone D Thompson
309 Wooddale Ave
New Castle DE 19720

Call Sign: KA3EPG
Norma J Wade
New Castle DE 19720

Call Sign: KA3KDW
John I Woodland
New Castle DE 19720

Call Sign: AA3IW
Wesley E Wade Sr
New Castle DE 19720

Call Sign: W3CH
Russell D Stafford
New Castle DE 197200426

Call Sign: W3PS
Metro Comm Repeater
System
New Castle DE 197200426

**FCC Amateur Radio
License in Newark**

Call Sign: WA3PJI
Martin J Brett Jr
5 Addison Dr
Newark DE 19702

Call Sign: AD3J
Martin J Brett Jr
5 Addison Dr
Newark DE 197021901

Call Sign: WB3AFN
Robert N Hackney
930 Alexandria Dr
Newark DE 19711

Call Sign: KB3PPB
Shura D Parks
5 Allandale Dr Apt E3
Newark DE 19713

Call Sign: KB3PWA

Mark A Parks
5 Allendale Dr Apt E3
Newark DE 19713

Call Sign: N3QNE
Tony N Gladwell Jr
74 Amstel Ave
Newark DE 19711

Call Sign: N3UQU
Charles E Hockersmith
1 Andries Rd
Newark DE 19711

Call Sign: N3CEH
Charles E Hockersmith
1 Andries Rd
Newark DE 19711

Call Sign: N3NGT
Deborah J Foster
5 Anita Dr
Newark DE 19713

Call Sign: WA3RAU
George T Reed
911 Aster Ave
Newark DE 19711

Call Sign: K3YEH
Harold W Fleischut Jr
27 Autumnwood Dr
Newark DE 19711

Call Sign: KB3RLL
Robert M Dunlap
152 Bartley Dr
Newark DE 19702

Call Sign: W2WOE
Robert M Dunlap
152 Bartley Dr
Newark DE 19702

Call Sign: KA3SRN

John R Bland
908 Baylor Dr
Newark DE 19711

Call Sign: N3FGP
Norman A Hare III
20 Beacon Ln
Newark DE 19711

Call Sign: K3ACE
Norman A Hare III
20 Beacon Ln
Newark DE 19711

Call Sign: WB3AKG
William F Nutter Jr
23 Beagle Club Way
Newark DE 19711

Call Sign: KB3GAL
Guido Viviano
11 Beech Hill Dr
Newark DE 19711

Call Sign: N3QNB
Todd M Mazur
68 Beech Hill Dr
Newark DE 19711

Call Sign: N3RNE
Lisa C Mazur
68 Beech Hill Dr
Newark DE 19711

Call Sign: NN3M
Stephen W Worden
117 Bent Ln
Newark DE 19711

Call Sign: KA3RME
Guy A Brooks
410 Beverly Rd
Newark DE 19711

Call Sign: KA3UJN

Chris M Carroll
18 Blue Fox Ct
Newark DE 19711

Call Sign: KB2OAS
Lawrence L Heidenberg
42 Blue Ridge Cir
Newark DE 19702

Call Sign: N3FFY
Edward C Ratledge
102 Brewster Dr
Newark DE 19711

Call Sign: K3CWF
Edward C Ratledge
102 Brewster Dr
Newark DE 19711

Call Sign: KB3YCL
Alexander B Schneider
2 Bristol Ct
Newark DE 19710

Call Sign: N3DNM
Ronald J Worden
26 Broadfield Dr
Newark DE 19713

Call Sign: N3QMZ
Roland J Wall
163 Brookside Blvd
Newark DE 19713

Call Sign: N3HGC
Peter D Moss
5302 Byron Ct
Newark DE 19711

Call Sign: N3HXF
Ronald Di Francis
101 Caladium Ln
Newark DE 19711

Call Sign: N3LOC

Donna L Di Francis
101 Caladium Ln
Newark DE 19711

Call Sign: KB3MML
David R Gerber
106 Caladium Ln
Newark DE 19711

Call Sign: KB3HG
Thomas P Carpenter
506 Cambridge Dr
Newark DE 197112704

Call Sign: N3GUL
Robert E Neeves
811 Cambridge Dr
Newark DE 19711

Call Sign: KB3GNM
Christopher R Kissell
1110 Capitol Trail
Newark DE 197113922

Call Sign: KB3CCS
Winston Griffith
8 Chambly Ct Forest Knoll
Newark DE 197024232

Call Sign: KA3KMD
Rodney C Doss
57 Chambord Dr
Newark DE 19702

Call Sign: N3OUT
Charles J Slezak
6 Charcoal Ct
Newark DE 19702

Call Sign: KB3FGI
Nancy E Black
6 Charcoal Ct
Newark DE 19702

Call Sign: N3QNF

George M Colbert
45 Cherokee Dr
Newark DE 19713

Call Sign: W3FXJ
Joseph F Duff Jr
25 Cheswald Blvd Apt 2C
Newark DE 19713

Call Sign: K3VYL
Robert H Clarke
709 Chrysler Ave
Newark DE 19711

Call Sign: KB3WLL
Edward R Adams
718 Chrysler Ave
Newark DE 19711

Call Sign: N3MJM
Leah L Pearl
2705 Cindy Dr
Newark DE 19702

Call Sign: KC7YBK
Ray W Ashby
6 Clear Spring Ln
Newark DE 19711

Call Sign: KB3FRR
Deborah L Dayton
11 Clover Ln
Newark DE 19713

Call Sign: WB4OSM
William P Wise
5 Cohansey Cir
Newark DE 19702

Call Sign: N3NGV
Curtis G Dell
211 Comet Ln
Newark DE 19711

Call Sign: KA3GRM

Rodney M Burge
544 Concord Bridge
Newark DE 19702

Call Sign: N3TXR
Kenneth C Pierce
7 Cordel
Newark DE 19711

Call Sign: NU3A
Kenneth C Pierce Jr
7 Cordele Dr
Newark DE 19711

Call Sign: KB3DDD
Richard H Duggan
44 Covered Bridge Ln
Newark DE 197112043

Call Sign: KB3EFO
Frank J Sciallo
311 Cox Rd
Newark DE 19711

Call Sign: KF4AXT
Craig A Reynolds
123 Creekmont Ct
Newark DE 19702

Call Sign: KB3WOY
Gregory Vermeychuk
717 Crossan Rd
Newark DE 19711

Call Sign: NZ3Y
Gregory Vermeychuk
717 Crossan Rd
Newark DE 19711

Call Sign: N3OXP
Matthew H Chamberlain
169 Darling St
Newark DE 19702

Call Sign: KB2WPC

William H Taylor
13 Darwin Rd
Newark DE 19702

Call Sign: N3DFY
George F Dunn
33 Decker Dr
Newark DE 19711

Call Sign: KA3OSJ
Herbert O Wardell Jr
37 Decker Dr
Newark DE 19711

Call Sign: KS3S
Ray R Schinzel
21 Devalinder Dr
Newark DE 19702

Call Sign: KB3PVZ
Donald A Stallings
443 Douglas D Alley Dr
Newark DE 19713

Call Sign: N3QHH
Benjamin F Powell III
4 Drexel Hall English
Village
Newark DE 19711

Call Sign: WB2PPY
Joel T Shertok
117 Drummond Farms Ln
Newark DE 197118323

Call Sign: N3MET
Apostolos Matulas
108 Duet Dr
Newark DE 19713

Call Sign: KA3WSZ
James R Phillips
402 Durso Dr
Newark DE 19711

Call Sign: KB3PD
Richard L Phillips
402 Durso Dr
Newark DE 19711

Call Sign: K3BVI
Stephen J Roberts
47 E Cleveland Ave
Newark DE 19711

Call Sign: KB3HMT
Clifford Barcliff
40 E Main St 250
Newark DE 19711

Call Sign: AA3ZQ
Clifford Barcliff
40 E Main St 250
Newark DE 19711

Call Sign: N3FJ
Clifford Barcliff
40 E Main St 250
Newark DE 19711

Call Sign: KB3MSH
Anuraag Mohan
334 E Main St N5
Newark DE 19711

Call Sign: N3TGO
Elizabeth A Robinson
12 E Periwinkle Ln
Newark DE 19711

Call Sign: N3TGP
Dale W Robinson
12 E Periwinkle Ln
Newark DE 19711

Call Sign: KB3SCM
Lloyd G Massey Jr
201 E Seneca Dr
Newark DE 19702

Call Sign: AF3LY
Lloyd G Massey Jr
201 E Seneca Dr
Newark DE 19702

Call Sign: N3MWR
Mohammad Arif
50 E Shady Dr
Newark DE 19713

Call Sign: WA3FQU
Allen W Pennell
223 Elderfield Rd
Newark DE 19713

Call Sign: N3JJR
Eric P Moyer
260 Elkton Rd D10
Newark DE 19711

Call Sign: KB3TGJ
Nicholas Waite
260 Elkton Rd G5
Newark DE 19711

Call Sign: W3UD
Amateur Rad Assoc At
The Univ Of Delaware
140 Evans Hall
Newark DE 19716

Call Sign: WB3EHC
Roger S Kauffman
27 Fall Brooke Rd
Newark DE 19711

Call Sign: N3UQR
Kathryn R Smith
105 Fantasia Dr
Newark DE 19713

Call Sign: N3WKW
Lynn H Smith
105 Fantasia Dr
Newark DE 19713

Call Sign: N3UKZ
James T Smith Jr
105 Fantasia Dr
Newark DE 197131903

Call Sign: KB3SIC
Stephen W Gouge
39 Gershwin Cir
Newark DE 19702

Call Sign: N3JPW
Carroll M Edgar
35 Greenridge Rd
Newark DE 19711

Call Sign: N3WDD
Michael B Smith
105 Fantasia Dr
Newark DE 197131903

Call Sign: N2QEB
William M Burbage
50 Gilbert Ct
Newark DE 19713

Call Sign: KB3UAV
Dawn S Edgar
35 Greenrodge Rd
Newark DE 19711

Call Sign: N3UZ
James T Smith Jr
105 Fantasia Dr
Newark DE 197131903

Call Sign: N3VRV
Rhonda K Davis
108 Gladstone Way
Newark DE 19702

Call Sign: WA3ZMO
H J Baylis
21 Gristmill Ln
Newark DE 197118003

Call Sign: KT3AN
Kathryn R Smith
105 Fantasia Dr
Newark DE 197131903

Call Sign: NY3C
Eugene L Mc Dowell
1705 Godwin Dr
Newark DE 19702

Call Sign: KA3DNF
Paul R Wells Jr
29 Gurnsey Dr
Newark DE 19713

Call Sign: KB3JUB
Scott L Mccarter
303 Fashion Cir
Newark DE 19711

Call Sign: KB3TI
Frederick F Publicover
24 Gogh Cir
Newark DE 19702

Call Sign: W4LQF
Paul R Wells Sr
29 Gurnsey Dr
Newark DE 19713

Call Sign: N3JCR
Daniel P Peters Jr
3259 Fraye Rd
Newark DE 19702

Call Sign: K3KIB
Frederick F Publicover
24 Gogh Cir
Newark DE 19702

Call Sign: N3IBC
Richard G Pyle
510 Hanna Dr E
Newark DE 19702

Call Sign: N3UTX
Norma L Peters
3259 Frazer Rd
Newark DE 19702

Call Sign: WA3QND
Clay A Will
1218 Grayrock Rd
Newark DE 19713

Call Sign: KB3OJN
Douglass F Taber
717 Harvard Ln
Newark DE 19711

Call Sign: N3JFS
Daniel P Peters III
3263 Frazer Rd
Newark DE 19702

Call Sign: KB3PMZ
G Eric Babcock
106 Great Cir Rd
Newark DE 19711

Call Sign: WB3CVN
Richard T Allen
807 Hastings Ct
Newark DE 197024090

Call Sign: KB3KRU
Melanie Peters
3263 Frazer Rd
Newark DE 19702

Call Sign: KB3VQM
Ryan J Cuga
9 Greenfield Ct
Newark DE 19713

Call Sign: KB3UNO
Charles J Cotton
3 Headwater Ln
Newark DE 19711

Call Sign: N3OWO
Jonathan D Hauke
46 Heather Rd
Newark DE 19702

Call Sign: KB2JKJ
Mason B Taube
61 Helios Ct
Newark DE 19711

Call Sign: N5FEL
Lonnie D Webb
2 Henderson Hill Rd
Newark DE 19711

Call Sign: N3TXS
Edwin D Stowell Jr
11 Holly Oak Dr
Newark DE 197131055

Call Sign: N3JVZ
William L Ross
12 Hollyoak Ln
Newark DE 19713

Call Sign: N3VUG
Frank Cc Savery
17 Independence Hall
English Village
Newark DE 19711

Call Sign: W3VOA
Robert E Picking
1309 Independence Way
Newark DE 197131169

Call Sign: N7DCM
Dorothy M Nonnemacher
244 Ingram St
Newark DE 19702

Call Sign: KB3PMY
Josef T Rubens
12 Ironwood Dr

Newark DE 19711

Call Sign: W3WWR
Josef T Rubens
12 Ironwood Dr
Newark DE 19711

Call Sign: K3QID
Thomas M Hanczyc
1001 Janice Dr
Newark DE 19713

Call Sign: KB3ONZ
Thomas J Gerard
21 Jarrell Farms Dr
Newark DE 19711

Call Sign: KA3ITA
John A Dean Jr
305 Jaymar Blvd
Newark DE 19702

Call Sign: WB3GOO
Jack A Lowe
12 Jobs Ln
Newark DE 19711

Call Sign: N3YPO
Eugene A Pappianne
35 Jonathan Dr
Newark DE 19711

Call Sign: KB3UXA
Suzan L Swartz
7 Juniper Dr
Newark DE 19702

Call Sign: KA1SLS
Suzan L Swartz
7 Juniper Dr
Newark DE 19702

Call Sign: WB2LOA
Harry M Brobst
206 Jupiter Rd

Newark DE 19711

Call Sign: WA3YWI
Charles F Barr
70 Kenmar Dr
Newark DE 19713

Call Sign: KB3WYH
Philip J Mcgovern
103 Kenmark Rd Todd Est
Newark DE 19713

Call Sign: KB3DOJ
David H Schmidt
710 Kilgor Ct
Newark DE 19702

Call Sign: N3NGS
Nada A Jones
106 Kingswood Rd
Newark DE 19713

Call Sign: W3DOL
John O Jones
1817.5 Kirkwood Hwy
Newark DE 19711

Call Sign: KF3CF
Richard J Mcguire
28 Kollman Dr
Newark DE 19713

Call Sign: KB3VQS
William L Halberstadt
505 Lark Dr
Newark DE 19713

Call Sign: W3WLH
William L Halberstadt
505 Lark Dr
Newark DE 19713

Call Sign: KB3FMY
Donald L Berry
11 Laurel Ave

Newark DE 197114797

Call Sign: KB3IZU
Betsy G Voss
11 Laurel Ave
Newark DE 19711

Call Sign: W3SKN
Donald L Berry
11 Laurel Ave
Newark DE 197114797

Call Sign: KB3PWB
John M Clancy
235 Laurel Ave
Newark DE 19711

Call Sign: N3CUJ
Andrew J Alvarez
57 Leader Dr
Newark DE 19713

Call Sign: N3DLW
Sharon C Alvarez
57 Leader Dr Newark
Oaks
Newark DE 19713

Call Sign: N3ZIF
Carlos Ortiz
1 Lilac Ct
Newark DE 19702

Call Sign: N2HJO
Karen L Russo
102 Lilac Way
Newark DE 19702

Call Sign: KA3JYU
Irwin J Drews
1137 Little Baltimore Rd
Newark DE 19711

Call Sign: N3DNE
Lena M Hubbard

1137 Little Baltimore Rd
Newark DE 19711

Call Sign: KB3OXC
Gene W Cole
12 Macduff Ct Abbotsford
Newark DE 19711

Call Sign: KB3VRG
Sharron S Boyle
26 Malvern Rd
Newark DE 19713

Call Sign: WB3CAG
Robert F Bashford
704 Manfield Rd
Newark DE 19713

Call Sign: AB3D
William A Mc Eachen Jr
1121 Maplefield Rd
Newark DE 197132412

Call Sign: WB3KDM
Albert O Neill Jr
14 Marabou Dr
Newark DE 19702

Call Sign: KA3HED
Gerard T Cichocki
212 Marabou Dr
Newark DE 19702

Call Sign: W3PCZ
Henry N Spears
308 Mason Dr
Newark DE 19711

Call Sign: KB3EAN
Mark A Pearson
38 Matthews Rd
Newark DE 19713

Call Sign: WB3GXD
Barry B Bogart

102 Mc Cann Rd
Newark DE 197116627

Call Sign: WB3HEW
Donald E Osborne Sr
121 Mc Cann Rd
Newark DE 19711

Call Sign: WA3DLH
William B Doyle
21 Mc Cord Dr
Newark DE 19713

Call Sign: N3CGH
Kathy Bogart
102 McCann Rd
Newark DE 19711

Call Sign: KA3OQR
Kurt W Wells
38 Meadow Ln
Newark DE 19713

Call Sign: WA3U
Stanley D Dabell
2 Memory Ln
Newark DE 19702

Call Sign: WK3Y
Alfred S De Luca Jr
232 Mercury Rd
Newark DE 19711

Call Sign: KA3LUR
Wayne S Purse
239 Mercury Rd
Newark DE 197113038

Call Sign: KB3LWD
Wayne S Purse
239 Mercury Rd
Newark DE 197113038

Call Sign: K3WSP
Wayne S Purse

239 Mercury Rd
Newark DE 197113038

Call Sign: W3WIL
William E Marcus
74 Midland Dr
Newark DE 19713

Call Sign: N3MZW
Charles N Boyle
1 Millbrook Rd
Newark DE 19713

Call Sign: KB3CRA
Roberto Lugo
2313 Milton Pl
Newark DE 19702

Call Sign: KB3UHW
Eunbok Lee
17 Montague Rd
Newark DE 19713

Call Sign: K3PGA
Eunbok Lee
17 Montague Rd
Newark DE 19713

Call Sign: N3YJF
Neilsen L Garrett
16 Mozart Way
Newark DE 19702

Call Sign: KB2TNQ
William D Staab
104 N Brownleaf
Newark DE 19713

Call Sign: KB3JOQ
Veronica D Raker
50 N Chapel St
Newark DE 19711

Call Sign: KC2ZDP
Kevin M Turner

703 N Country Club Dr
Newark DE 19711

Call Sign: N3FIW
Dennis G Cripps
218 N Dillwyn Rd
Newark DE 19711

Call Sign: KB2GCG
Gerald Simonowits
165 N Hunter Forge Rd
Newark DE 19713

Call Sign: W3JKS
John K Scoggin Jr
500 N Wakefield Dr
Newark DE 197146066

Call Sign: KA3BXN
Robert P Hagerty
15 Needleleaf Dr
Newark DE 19702

Call Sign: KB3PUY
Adalberto T Castelo
3 Nethy Dr
Newark DE 197111525

Call Sign: KB3PVB
Ellen M Phifer
3 Nethy Dr
Newark DE 197111525

Call Sign: KA3OGV
Maria G Murphy
2 New Casho Mill Rd
Newark DE 19711

Call Sign: KF3AQ
Axel T Wittich
10 North St
Newark DE 19711

Call Sign: N3AHY
Milton Landis

239 Oakfield Dr
Newark DE 197132445

Call Sign: N3FHL
Dean R Dungan
253 Oakfield Dr
Newark DE 19713

Call Sign: KA3DGC
H Edwin Kennedy
2855 Ogletown Rd
Newark DE 19713

Call Sign: KE4CRM
Michael E Callanan
4142 Ogletown Stanton Rd
412
Newark DE 19713

Call Sign: KA3WOM
Paul J Riley
127 Old Baltimore Pike
Newark DE 19702

Call Sign: KA3TKO
Marybeth K Miller
1521 Old Coach Rd
Newark DE 19711

Call Sign: WB3KIS
Mark L Miller Sr
1521 Old Coach Rd
Newark DE 19711

Call Sign: KB3ROJ
Michael W Raymond
40 Old Farm Rd
Newark DE 19711

Call Sign: N3MWR
Michael W Raymond
40 Old Farm Rd
Newark DE 19711

Call Sign: KB3GVC

John P Mikus
14 Old Fence Ln
Newark DE 197023719

Call Sign: N8ZUG
Nathan M Zedan
49 Old Fence Ln
Newark DE 19702

Call Sign: KA3UME
Jeffrey R Ramberg
18 Old Manor Rd
Newark DE 19711

Call Sign: WD6EQZ
Paul M Hodgson Jr
302 Old Oak Rd
Newark DE 19711

Call Sign: KB3OCU
John A Billon
401 Old Oak Rd
Newark DE 19711

Call Sign: WA3UZR
Merle A Roemer Sr
937 Otts Chapel Rd
Newark DE 19713

Call Sign: N1BIL
William E Marcus
1632 Otts Chapel Rd
Newark DE 19702

Call Sign: N3HBA
Vernon W Brown Jr
750 Paper Mill Rd
Newark DE 19711

Call Sign: KB3VBA
C F Mann
1 Paul Ct
Newark DE 197022846

Call Sign: KB3VFN

Sonseeree G Gardner
560 Peoples Plaza Ste 176
Newark DE 19702

Call Sign: N3ZWW
Shawn H Rullens
154 Petal Pl
Newark DE 19702

Call Sign: KA3DQD
Shawn H Rullens
154 Petal Pl
Newark DE 19702

Call Sign: N3FDL
Michael Witkowski
17 Phoenix Ave
Newark DE 19702

Call Sign: WA3QHJ
Patrick W Horner
30 Phoenix Ave
Newark DE 19702

Call Sign: KB3SCL
Phillip B Dingus
14 Pinedale Rd
Newark DE 19711

Call Sign: WB3GTU
Mary W Ingersoll
219 Planet Rd N Star
Newark DE 19711

Call Sign: KA3AYP
Betty F Thorp
2078 Pleasant Valley Rd
Newark DE 19702

Call Sign: WB3ISU
Francis R Thorp
2078 Pleasant Valley Rd
Newark DE 19702

Call Sign: KB3CQN

Phil B Burkley
PO Box 9235
Newark DE 19714

Call Sign: KB3POZ
Maurice J Moudy
441 Polly Drummond Hill
Rd
Newark DE 19711

Call Sign: K3MJM
Maurice J Moudy
441 Polly Drummond Hill
Rd
Newark DE 19711

Call Sign: KA3VOW
Bruce A Meck
619 Postfield Rd Scottfield
Newark DE 19713

Call Sign: KB3DUP
Greg A Aluise
13 Prescott Dr
Newark DE 19702

Call Sign: W3DIB
Greg A Aluise
13 Prescott Dr
Newark DE 19702

Call Sign: N3RNI
Richard J Rossi
15 Quartz Mill Rd
Newark DE 19711

Call Sign: KA3IQL
Parker E Dean
4 Quentin Hall
Newark DE 19711

Call Sign: N2CAF
Gary B Pizzolo
8 Rankin Rd
Newark DE 19711

Call Sign: N3GLG
Amy L Klein
Red Fox Ln
Newark DE 19711

Call Sign: KB3SLV
Joseph J Rollo Jr
12 Regal Ct
Newark DE 19713

Call Sign: KB3CTQ
Yves R Hartmann
127 Register Dr
Newark DE 19711

Call Sign: N3WGP
Ralph S Culver
29 Renee Ln
Newark DE 19711

Call Sign: KF3DU
Ralph S Culver
29 Renee Ln
Newark DE 19711

Call Sign: AA3VV
Ralph S Culver
29 Renee Ln
Newark DE 19711

Call Sign: K3IKY
Frederick Kirch
7 Ridgewood Turn
Newark DE 19711

Call Sign: N3MEW
Robert E Rockey
119 Rolling Dr
Newark DE 19713

Call Sign: KB3RUU
Jack A Puleo
2 Rossiter Cir
Newark DE 19702

Call Sign: KB3PKZ
Kenneth G Mcneil
22 Running Brook Ln
Newark DE 19711

Call Sign: N3KSC
Edward T Burke Jr
235 S Chapel St
Newark DE 19711

Call Sign: W3DNN
Joseph F Hayes
114 S Dillwyn Rd
Newark DE 19711

Call Sign: WA3UGN
Franz H Noll
231 S Dillwyn Rd Windy
Hills
Newark DE 19711

Call Sign: N3YH
Edward W Schwinger
257 S Thistle Way
Newark DE 19702

Call Sign: K3WMS
Wendy M Kapochus
257 S Thistle Way
Newark DE 19702

Call Sign: AB3FS
Edward W Schwinger
257 S Thistle Way
Newark DE 19702

Call Sign: KB3PKE
Wendy M Kapochus
257 S Thistle Way
Newark DE 19702

Call Sign: WA2GZI
Peter N Black
2104 S way Dr

Newark DE 19713

Call Sign: KB3FME
Rapp W Crook
8 Saddle Cir
Newark DE 197112007

Call Sign: KA3CFH
Thomas C Wool
20 Saint Regis Dr
Newark DE 19711

Call Sign: W3BM
William A Mason
1001 Sandburg Pl
Newark DE 197024435

Call Sign: N3HOU
Joseph F Rullens
120 Scottfield Dr
Newark DE 19713

Call Sign: WA3DUM
James E Hicks
185 Scottfield Dr
Newark DE 19713

Call Sign: KB3RUV
Chet K Hadley
6 Shade Ct
Newark DE 19702

Call Sign: W4SWR
Deni S Galileo
20 Sheldon Dr
Newark DE 19711

Call Sign: W3QQ
Cedrick D Justis
49 Shields Ln
Newark DE 197023110

Call Sign: KB3IUL
Michael J Manning
626 Slate Dr

Newark DE 19702

Call Sign: KA3WOO
Robert C Elliott
31 Spectrum Dr
Newark DE 19713

Call Sign: WB3BAM
William C Pitts
126 Spruce Glen Dr
Newark DE 19711

Call Sign: AA3LU
John R Bodzo
209 Spruce Glen Dr
Newark DE 19711

Call Sign: KA3WON
Oral P Moore
150 Spruceglen Dr
Newark DE 19711

Call Sign: N3KDF
Catherine J Black
100 St Regis Dr
Newark DE 19711

Call Sign: N3FQB
John M Iannarella Jr
4 Stallion Dr
Newark DE 19713

Call Sign: W3TZI
Paul E Eriksen
13 Stalwart Dr
Newark DE 19713

Call Sign: N3SKO
John K Scoggin Jr
4142 Stanton-Ogletown Rd
Ms 215
Newark DE 19713

Call Sign: N3MZX
Edward P Seichepine

20 Stature Dr
Newark DE 19713

Call Sign: KA3CRX
Nancy L Voss
40 Stature Dr
Newark DE 19713

Call Sign: N3ACA
Stanley M Voss
40 Stature Dr Sherwood Fr
Newark DE 19713

Call Sign: KK4BA
Edward M Simmons
3201 Stone Pl
Newark DE 19702

Call Sign: KA3MOX
Matthew C Bucklen
1015 Summit View Dr
Newark DE 197131129

Call Sign: N3EBF
Frank E South
208 Sunset Rd
Newark DE 19711

Call Sign: KB3WQH
Robert J Dobie
526 Tamara Cir
Newark DE 19711

Call Sign: KB3IML
Edward C Brown Jr
8 Tenby Chase Dr
Newark DE 19711

Call Sign: W3HCF
David L Mills
43 The Horseshoe
Newark DE 19711

Call Sign: N3SET
Richard J Seibel

13 Timber Creek Ln
Newark DE 19711

Call Sign: KB3SQJ
Daniel R Vincent
19 Timberline Dr
Newark DE 19711

Call Sign: N3DQI
Phillip R De Courcelle Jr
11 Tiverton Cir
Newark DE 19702

Call Sign: KB3MZQ
John J Krajewski
30 Tiverton Cir
Newark DE 19702

Call Sign: KB3NTJ
Kathy A Krajewski
30 Tiverton Cir
Newark DE 19702

Call Sign: KB3PZN
James W Campbell
10 Trevett Blvd
Newark DE 19702

Call Sign: WA3EWK
Robert Averitt
1004 Tulip Tree Ln
Newark DE 19713

Call Sign: N3WBH
David M Dempsey
28 Upland Ct
Newark DE 19713

Call Sign: KA3JUJ
Mark A Stillman
48 Upland Ct
Newark DE 19713

Call Sign: KB3YEZ
Wendell D Harvey

61 Upland Ct
Newark DE 19713

16 Verdi Cr
Newark DE 19702

211 Welsh Tract Rd 80
Newark DE 19713

Call Sign: N3WTA
Charles A Mc Laren Jr
5 Vassar Dr
Newark DE 19711

Call Sign: AB3PK
Peter J Cassells
284 W Chestnut Hill Rd
Newark DE 19713

Call Sign: N5PTF
Kunchit Chamaraman
214 Wharton Dr
Newark DE 19711

Call Sign: KB3PUA
Stephen Howard
404 Vassar Dr
Newark DE 19711

Call Sign: KA3IQG
Diane Lowry
403 W Hanna Dr
Newark DE 19702

Call Sign: KB3VMB
Thip Nakchum
214 Wharton Dr
Newark DE 19711

Call Sign: KB1KCY
Jose F Lugo Jr
113 Venus Dr
Newark DE 197113019

Call Sign: WB2LSP
William R Lowry
403 W Hanna Dr
Newark DE 19702

Call Sign: KB3HCV
Adam R Markey
808 Wharton Dr
Newark DE 19711

Call Sign: WN8RQC
Michael A Kerezsi
1 Verdant Cir
Newark DE 19702

Call Sign: KB3REU
Michael Federico
52 W Kyla Marie Dr
Newark DE 197025431

Call Sign: KB3DFL
Arvind Narayanaswamy
1117 Wharton Dr
Newark DE 197163726

Call Sign: W3ASW
Michael J Kerezsi
1 Verdant Cir
Newark DE 19702

Call Sign: KB3PTL
Ellen Z Ellis
168 W Park Pl
Newark DE 19711

Call Sign: KB3DZ
George S Coble Jr
27 White Dr
Newark DE 19702

Call Sign: WB8MRU
Michael J Kerezsi Jr
1 Verdant Ct
Newark DE 19702

Call Sign: N3VXS
Stephen D Potter
17 W Stephen Dr
Newark DE 19713

Call Sign: W4EAZ
George S Coble Jr
27 White Dr
Newark DE 19702

Call Sign: KB3PKD
Mark S Robinson
9 Verdant Ct
Newark DE 19702

Call Sign: KB3PKY
William W John
362 Wallace Dr
Newark DE 19711

Call Sign: WB2NHJ
Janice A Masciarelli
Windsor Cir
Newark DE 19702

Call Sign: KB3NYE
Chris R Knotts
16 Verdi Cr
Newark DE 19702

Call Sign: KA3TXJ
Paula S Shulak
211 Welsh Tract Rd 80
Newark DE 19713

Call Sign: KB3REV
Robert M Gentile
509 Windsor Dr
Newark DE 19711

Call Sign: KN0TTS
Chris R Knotts

Call Sign: NS3G
Carl A Shulak

Call Sign: N3NRG
Robert M Gentile

509 Windsor Dr
Newark DE 19711

Call Sign: KB3GHQ
Paul V Eldridge
19 Winnwood Rd
Newark DE 197115553

Call Sign: N3OWQ
Zanetta M Norris
2909 Winterhaven Dr
Newark DE 19702

Call Sign: KB3CAJ
Steven A Kauffman
720 Wollaston Ave
Newark DE 197115114

Call Sign: WB9TXT
Tony S Freedman
60 Woodhill Ct
Newark DE 19711

Call Sign: KA3VZE
Bruce E Fisher
102 Worral Dr
Newark DE 19711

Call Sign: WA2IPT
William H Gray
12 Yancey Ln
Newark DE 19702

Call Sign: WB3FUP
Michael F Hall
1103 Yellowstone Dr
Newark DE 19713

Call Sign: WB2TLO
John C Miller
Newark DE 19711

Call Sign: K3DX
David W Drew
Newark DE 19715

Call Sign: N3DEL
Hi Tech Rednecks
Newark DE 197148030

Call Sign: N3TU
Gregory T Cowchok
Newark DE 19714

Call Sign: WB2YKS
John P Biaselli
Newark DE 19714

Call Sign: N3WEP
Christopher W Drew
Newark DE 19715

Call Sign: N3XZG
Robert P Mc Kenzie
Newark DE 19715

Call Sign: NN9G
Hi Tech Rednecks
Newark DE 197148030

Call Sign: K3QBD
First State Amateur Radio
Club Inc
Newark DE 197151050

Call Sign: KB3RUT
Thomas E Mckenna
Newark DE 19714

Call Sign: N3TGR
Kathleen E Joseph
201 E Justis St
Newport DE 198042521

Call Sign: KB3PZV

New Castle County
Emergency Operations
Group
107 Lincoln Ave
Newport DE 19804

Call Sign: W3GLM
Gail L Mc Cray
107 Lincoln Ave
Newport DE 19804

Call Sign: W3RSM
Robin S Mc Cray
107 Lincoln Ave
Newport DE 19804

Call Sign: WA3DUH
James W Hicks
217 W Ayre St
Newport DE 19804

Call Sign: N3NMO
Frank P Bryson
18 Amandas Way
Ocean View DE 19970

Call Sign: K3GUX
Joseph V Hartman Sr
37706 Balsa St
Ocean View DE 19970

Call Sign: N3HIE
Joseph Gualtieri
Box 323
Ocean View DE 19970

Call Sign: KA3HAE
Hayward R Daisey
Box 66
Ocean View DE 19970

Call Sign: N3FGX

Joyce A Daisey
Box 66
Ocean View DE 19970

Call Sign: KA3T
Richard A White Jr
8 Carly Ct
Ocean View DE 19970

Call Sign: KB3OKY
Jonathan E Rogers
588 Central Ave
Ocean View DE 19970

Call Sign: KA3TCG
Carroll W Cooper
23 Clover Ln
Ocean View DE
199701337

Call Sign: KB3HCJ
Frank L Blunda
15 Columbia Ave
Ocean View DE 19970

Call Sign: KB3TXV
Zachary F Richard
10 Cromwell
Ocean View DE 19970

Call Sign: KB3TXS
David K Ryan
31806 Good Earth Ln
Ocean View DE 19970

Call Sign: N3TCW
Pauline E Barcus
24 Kent Ave
Ocean View DE 19970

Call Sign: N3LIS
Vaughn R Parfitt
314 N Orlando Ave
Ocean View DE
199709760

Call Sign: N3QJI
Wayne A Stacey
75 Velta Dr
Ocean View DE
199700784

Call Sign: KB3HTQ
Michael R Stacey
38490 Velta Dr
Ocean View DE 19970

Call Sign: N3GTJ
James L Machamer
Ocean View DE 19970

Call Sign: N3NNB
Mary T Rothwell
Ocean View DE 19970

Call Sign: W3CDY
Lloyd W Sherman
Ocean View DE 19970

Call Sign: N3TVU
William A Olsen
Ocean View DE
199701368

Call Sign: KB3UKE
Kenneth R Hooker Sr
Ocean View DE 19970

FCC Amateur Radio License in Odessa

Call Sign: N1XAU
Bridget A Wyrick
108 Front St
Odessa DE 19730

Call Sign: N1UC
Charles L Wyrick
108 Front St
Odessa DE 197300167

FCC Amateur Radio License in Port Penn

Call Sign: KR1KEN
Kenneth G Kirk
Port Penn DE 197310181

FCC Amateur Radio License in Rehobeth Beach

Call Sign: WB3KAB
Robert J Di Pasquale
20 Arnell Dr
Rehobeth Beach DE
199719699

Call Sign: KB3MZO
Paul Petren
10 Kings Creek Cir
Rehobeth Beach DE 19971

Call Sign: AA3BQ
Harry J Crowley
24 Tiffany Dr
Rehobeth Beach DE 19971

Call Sign: KA3NYI
Randall E Kobetich
4 Wood Dr
Rehobeth Beach DE 19971

Call Sign: KA2AYN
Matthew W Kehoe
37391 4th St
Rehoboth Beach DE 19971

Call Sign: KB3OLC
Benjamin D Edmonds
113 Beachfield Dr
Rehoboth Beach DE 19971

Call Sign: KG4MBP
F William Pfordt

25521 Bishop Bend
Rehoboth Beach DE 19971

21237 K St
Rehoboth Beach DE 19971

205 Stockley St
Rehoboth Beach DE 19971

Call Sign: W3YTW
Winfield S Standiford III
13 Breakwater Dr
Rehoboth Beach DE 19971

Call Sign: WA8JCP
Russell W Frum
10 Kendal Ln
Rehoboth Beach DE 19971

Call Sign: WA2BHB
Michael R Strange
6 Stockley St
Rehoboth Beach DE 19971

Call Sign: WA3UUO
Denton C Aylor
8 Cavendish Ct
Rehoboth Beach DE 19971

Call Sign: KE0HK
James E Morrison Jr
18 Kingsbridge Rd
Rehoboth Beach DE 19971

Call Sign: KB3VXZ
Robert A Wilson
28 Virginia Ave
Rehoboth Beach DE 19971

Call Sign: W3KS
Denton C Aylor
8 Cavendish Ct
Rehoboth Beach DE 19971

Call Sign: N3BTL
Norma H Daisey
101 Kingsbridge Rd
Rehoboth Beach DE 19971

Call Sign: N3ELN
George J Danforth
61 W Side Rd
Rehoboth Beach DE 19971

Call Sign: KB3MJ
Dennis V Karol
2 Club House Dr
Rehoboth Beach DE 19971

Call Sign: WB3HKW
Clifton J Daisey
101 Kingsbridge Rd
Rehoboth Beach DE 19971

Call Sign: KB3MJM
Joseph A Dipietrantonio
18 Wanoma Cir
Rehoboth Beach DE 19971

Call Sign: KA3GNC
Carol A Karol
2 Clubhouse Dr
Rehoboth Beach DE 19971

Call Sign: KC3JM
Jay F Leibforth
113 Martin Ln
Rehoboth Beach DE 19971

Call Sign: W3JDP
Joseph A Dipietrantonio
18 Wanoma Cir
Rehoboth Beach DE 19971

Call Sign: W3CAC
George W Calhoun
50 Delaware Ave
Rehoboth Beach DE 19971

Call Sign: KB3VXY
Jeffrey S Schoap
1 Ocean Breeze Dr
Rehoboth Beach DE 19971

Call Sign: W3GQK
Joseph F Mc Donnell III
45 Wanoma Cir
Rehoboth Beach DE 19971

Call Sign: N3IME
Robert A Streimer
154 Henlopen Ave
Rehoboth Beach DE 19971

Call Sign: WA3YTB
Bert S Lockard
7 Sabrina Dr
Rehoboth Beach DE 19971

Call Sign: AB3OF
Barry J Bauer
38291 William F St
Rehoboth Beach DE 19971

Call Sign: KA3LWJ
Harry A Becker
17 James A St
Rehoboth Beach DE 19971

Call Sign: N3CGO
John F Hyde
123 St Lawrence St
Rehoboth Beach DE 19971

Call Sign: N3HZH
Malcolm R Judkins
Rehoboth Beach DE 19971

Call Sign: KB3SYS
Francis P Antonio
Rehoboth Beach DE 19971

Call Sign: N3YVN
Vincent Palace

Call Sign: W3IUM
Edward F Ward

FCC Amateur Radio License in Rockland

Call Sign: KA3CNE
Benjamin F Du Pont
7 Rockland Meadows Rd
Rockland DE 19732

FCC Amateur Radio License in Roxana

Call Sign: W2LTP
Alfred A Greenberg
RR 2 Box 92Aa
Roxana DE 19945

FCC Amateur Radio License in Saint Georges

Call Sign: AC3T
Leonard K Moncaleri
720 Elizabeth Ln
Saint Georges DE
197330243

Call Sign: N3AYE
Ruth E Moncaleri
720 Elizabeth Ln
Saint Georges DE 19733

Call Sign: KA3SBP
Clifford C Widdekind
2 Hybridge Ave
Saint Georges DE 19733

Call Sign: N3AHC
Robert L Welch
110 W Harvest Dr
Saint Georges DE 19720

Call Sign: KB3ISB
Lewis D Harris
Saint Georges DE 19733

FCC Amateur Radio License in Seaford

Call Sign: KB3NRB
Trey Smith
7754 Arminger Dr
Seaford DE 19973

Call Sign: KB3HTB
Henry V Mancus Jr
6958 Atlanta Cir
Seaford DE 19973

Call Sign: N3YMK
Julie A Linek
1215 Atlanta Rd
Seaford DE 19973

Call Sign: KB3TXR
Shannon L Lecates
12798 Baker Mill Rd
Seaford DE 19973

Call Sign: KB3AMY
Michael D Cohen
12047 Baker Mill Rd
Seaford DE 19973

Call Sign: KB3HTL
Barbara R Hancock
20 Barley Run
Seaford DE 19973

Call Sign: KB3GAQ
Del Mar Va Dx
Association
20 Barley Run
Seaford DE 19973

Call Sign: W3IJ
Vaughn B Russell
22866 Bloxom School Rd
Seaford DE 19973

Call Sign: N3YMM

Jeffrey A Hancock
Box 20
Seaford DE 199739701

Call Sign: N3LGP
Mark J O Bier
Box 208D
Seaford DE 19973

Call Sign: N3LGL
Lloyd G Dabell
Box 231A
Seaford DE 19973

Call Sign: KC3UM
Walter W Osborne
Box 256F
Seaford DE 19973

Call Sign: WA2KZF
Glenn C Ward
Box 316A Concord
Seaford DE 19973

Call Sign: N3XKH
Lenora A Shankweiler
Box 364 Aa
Seaford DE 19973

Call Sign: NY3N
Raymond B Shankweiler
Sr
Box 364Aa
Seaford DE 19973

Call Sign: NQ3Q
Marvin L Bannon
Box 47
Seaford DE 19973

Call Sign: N3LKX
Quentin V Welch
Box 58
Seaford DE 19973

Call Sign: KB3LHH
James D Milam
20730 Bucks Branch Rd
Seaford DE 19973

Call Sign: KB3HTE
Marvin D Stumbo Sr
26540 Butler Branch Rd
Seaford DE 19973

Call Sign: KB3SKR
Mary J Yarnell
25545 Chevrolet Ave
Seaford DE 19973

Call Sign: N3ZNZ
Ernest S Hudson
5 Clover Dr
Seaford DE 19973

Call Sign: N3LNC
Steven M Collins
1404 Concord Rd
Seaford DE 19973

Call Sign: KF3AH
Robert L Taylor
2008 Concord Rd
Seaford DE 19973

Call Sign: N3EZY
James F Richardson
8559 Concord Rd
Seaford DE 199734277

Call Sign: KB3RJR
Nathan C Truitt
12900 Concord Rd
Seaford DE 19973

Call Sign: KB3NRW
Josh Dill
14596 Concord Rt 20
Seaford DE 19973

Call Sign: KB3JBQ
Marvin D Stumbo Jr
26193 Deely St
Seaford DE 19973

Call Sign: N3LNS
James D Osborne
26956 Dillards Rd
Seaford DE 19973

Call Sign: KB3FXF
Kristen D Ockels
26956 Dillards Rd
Seaford DE 19973

Call Sign: KB3SCZ
Tobias J Cerillo
208 E 6th St
Seaford DE 19973

Call Sign: N3WVP
George W Felton
724 E Ivory Dr
Seaford DE 19973

Call Sign: KB3CIZ
Carolyn E Smith
417 E Poplar St
Seaford DE 19973

Call Sign: KB3SPU
Johnathan R Lowe
410 E Popular St
Seaford DE 19973

Call Sign: N3YML
Leroy M Johns
900 Easter Ln H17
Seaford DE 19973

Call Sign: K3XV
Joseph J Walsh
5647 Edna Ave
Seaford DE 19973

Call Sign: KD4NSY
Gary L Hoops
5697 Edna Ave
Seaford DE 19973

Call Sign: N3NSY
Gary L Hoops
5697 Edna Ave
Seaford DE 19973

Call Sign: W3BEZ
Charles H Wall
8980 Elks Rd
Seaford DE 19973

Call Sign: KA3TVM
Judy A Bernstein
300 Elm Dr
Seaford DE 19973

Call Sign: KD3IG
Nicholas Bernstein
300 Elm Dr
Seaford DE 19973

Call Sign: KB3DTT
Parris S Mancuso
508 Elm Dr
Seaford DE 19973

Call Sign: KB3GMI
Thomas C Mancuso
508 Elm Dr
Seaford DE 19973

Call Sign: KB3JBU
Emmalee M B Mancuso
508 Elm Dr
Seaford DE 19973

Call Sign: K3JD
Richard A Cain
22351 Eskridge Rd
Seaford DE 19973

Call Sign: KD5FWV
Jessica A Starkey
7675 Grace Cir
Seaford DE 19973

Call Sign: N1MJC
Marian J Collier
25483 Jamie Ct
Seaford DE 199738310

Call Sign: N3FIA
James N Guthrie
2104 Middleford Rd
Seaford DE 19973

Call Sign: KB3OIN
Steve Bailey
4414 Green Briar Way
Seaford DE 19973

Call Sign: KB3QAU
James V Crescenzo
14040 Jana Cir E
Seaford DE 19973

Call Sign: KB3TXX
William B Holston
9963 Middleford Rd
Seaford DE 19973

Call Sign: N3WDK
Wendy B Bernstein
134 Hall St N
Seaford DE 19973

Call Sign: KA3IXU
Joseph J Walsh
100 Johnsons Dr
Seaford DE 19973

Call Sign: KB3SDI
Myles J Gray
917 N Atlanta Cir
Seaford DE 19973

Call Sign: KA3WIV
Jerry A Jones
7252 Hearns Pond Rd
Seaford DE 19973

Call Sign: KB3NRJ
Kassy Legates
23954 Kenmore Rd
Seaford DE 19973

Call Sign: N3SVB
Keith E Hertzog
306 N Bradford St
Seaford DE 19973

Call Sign: KD3GD
Susan A Osborne
22040 Hensley Rd
Seaford DE 19973

Call Sign: W3JSQ
Roland O Downes
7636 Kings Ct
Seaford DE 19973

Call Sign: N3TMG
Marian M Paul
306 N Bradford St
Seaford DE 19973

Call Sign: KV3D
Richard D Osborne
22040 Hensley Rd
Seaford DE 19973

Call Sign: KA1WVV
Brian J Bard
26839 Malihorn Dr
Seaford DE 199734756

Call Sign: KG4JLN
Tiffany M Paul
306 N Bradford St
Seaford DE 19973

Call Sign: KB3CWC
Michael W Blaine
25110 Holly Rd
Seaford DE 19973

Call Sign: WA3LSN
James O Warren Jr
313 Manticoke Ave
Seaford DE 19973

Call Sign: KG4JLO
Taylor H Paul
306 N Bradford St
Seaford DE 19973

Call Sign: KA3TVO
Charles D Dochtermann
810 Huston St
Seaford DE 19973

Call Sign: KB3MJR
Bradley C Snyder
4 Marathon Dr
Seaford DE 19973

Call Sign: N3WYN
Daniel J Braunstein
2 N Market Ext
Seaford DE 19973

Call Sign: WW3DE
Eric R Lindquist
25483 Jamie Ct
Seaford DE 19973

Call Sign: AC4TD
William L Brunner
2101 Middleford Rd
Seaford DE 19973

Call Sign: N3WYO
Seth D Braunstein
2 N Market Ext
Seaford DE 19973

Call Sign: KB3HTA
Laurel H Braunstein
2 N Market St Ext
Seaford DE 19973

Call Sign: KB3JGB
Herbert H Quick
25141 Oak Rd
Seaford DE 19973

Call Sign: K3TLG
Joseph H Gardner
106 Rivershore Dr
Seaford DE 19973

Call Sign: WB3HKY
John J Moran
29481 N Oak Grove Rd
Seaford DE 19973

Call Sign: KB3HTM
Dennis J Smith
807 Park Dr
Seaford DE 19973

Call Sign: N3AJY
Kay S Rudo
7519 Rivershore Dr
Seaford DE 19973

Call Sign: KA3SMS
Romeo A Escaro
27 N Shore Dr
Seaford DE 19973

Call Sign: K3DJS
Dennis J Smith
807 Park Dr
Seaford DE 19973

Call Sign: NJ3O
Mark R Rudo
7519 Rivershore Dr
Seaford DE 19973

Call Sign: N3END
Jose L Barriocanal
9709 N Shore Dr
Seaford DE 19973

Call Sign: N3MBB
Ingrid E Stafford
213 Paula Lynne Dr
Seaford DE 19973

Call Sign: WB3JTQ
Paul E Wolpert
26521 Riverview Cir
Seaford DE 199734330

Call Sign: K3VMX
William T Windley
418 N Willey St
Seaford DE 199732216

Call Sign: AA3TS
Quentin V Welch
26603 River Rd
Seaford DE 19973

Call Sign: KB3UVC
Samuel J Mitchell
6915 Robin Dr
Seaford DE 19973

Call Sign: N3GIL
Kenneth R Varell Jr
758 Nylon Blvd
Seaford DE 19973

Call Sign: N3LNV
David A Ingalls
18 Rivers End Dr
Seaford DE 19973

Call Sign: N3KBU
John M Gunson
125 S Paula Lynne Dr
Seaford DE 199739493

Call Sign: KB3RAR
Jocelyn K Quick
25141 Oak Rd
Seaford DE 19973

Call Sign: N3LNW
Kristin E Ingalls
18 Rivers End Dr
Seaford DE 19973

Call Sign: KB3IGA
Kenneth J Jager
28107 S Pine Ridge Dr
Seaford DE 19973

Call Sign: KB3UVE
Edward G Rollins
25146 Oak Rd
Seaford DE 19973

Call Sign: NW3Y
Charles C Allen III
55 Rivers End Dr
Seaford DE 199738008

Call Sign: K4CTD
Henri J Blair
301 S Winding Brooke Dr
Seaford DE 19973

Call Sign: KF3BT
Herbert G Quick
25141 Oak Rd
Seaford DE 19973

Call Sign: N3VPK
James S Anderson
90 Rivers End Dr
Seaford DE 199739696

Call Sign: N3OCU
William N Brown
26372 Seaford Rd
Seaford DE 19973

Call Sign: KB3JUO
George F Cranston
300 Shipley St
Seaford DE 19973

Call Sign: AA3KE
Sean P Ryan
905 Short Ln
Seaford DE 19973

Call Sign: KW3Z
Patrick W Ryan
905 Short Ln
Seaford DE 19973

Call Sign: N3VQG
Eric W Ryan
905 Short Ln
Seaford DE 19973

Call Sign: N3XOS
Georgia E Ryan
905 Short Ln
Seaford DE 19973

Call Sign: AA3ZP
Eric W Ryan
905 Short Ln
Seaford DE 19973

Call Sign: KX3I
Sean P Ryan
905 Short Ln
Seaford DE 19973

Call Sign: KE4BKV
David E Hasulak
21 Sussex Ct
Seaford DE 19973

Call Sign: KB3JUP
Jeffrey Moya
22167 Thompson Pkwy
Seaford DE 19973

Call Sign: N3GJN
David D Osborne
22 Thompson Pky
Seaford DE 19973

Call Sign: N3LNU
Kendora A Leifert
22 Thompson Pky
Seaford DE 19973

Call Sign: KB3TXL
Priyen M Patel
33 Tidewater Dr
Seaford DE 19973

Call Sign: KC4IHX
Martha C Mancuso
1408 Tomlinson Dr
Seaford DE 19973

Call Sign: W3PAR
Parris S Mancuso
1408 Tomlinson Dr
Seaford DE 19973

Call Sign: KB3OKW
Brandon M Norman
212 Tulip Pl
Seaford DE 19973

Call Sign: KB3CRK
Richard A Webb
508 Turkey Branch Rd
Seaford DE 19973

Call Sign: KB3HTR
Patrick R Parker
9730 Walnut Dr
Seaford DE 19973

Call Sign: KB3JUX
Ian M Mason
20349 Wesley Church Rd
Seaford DE 19973

Call Sign: KB3RAS
Donald G Taylor
26948 Windsor St
Seaford DE 19973

Call Sign: N3DTG
Donald G Taylor
26948 Windsor St
Seaford DE 19973

Call Sign: N3QJK
Paul L Bishop III
917 Wythe Ln
Seaford DE 19973

Call Sign: N3TKM
James A Hill II
Seaford DE 19973

Call Sign: N3YPN
Russell Horsey Jr
Seaford DE 19973

Call Sign: W3TBG
Nanticoke Amateur Radio
Club Inc
Seaford DE 19973

Call Sign: WV8RS
Ronnie W Starkey Jr
Seaford DE 19973

Call Sign: KB3OKZ
Schuyler V Livingston
Seaford DE 19973

**FCC Amateur Radio
License in Shelbyville**

Call Sign: N3SBD
Jeffrey R Hudson
1 Barn Owl Dr
Selbyville DE 19975

Call Sign: N3NSP

John A Webb Jr
2 Barn Owl Dr
Selbyville DE 19975

Call Sign: N3RKY
Richard A Mc Call
Box 142A
Selbyville DE 19975

Call Sign: N3NLP
Earllaine M Simpler
Box 20
Selbyville DE 19975

Call Sign: KB3JUN
Jeffrey K Collins
Box 31 D
Selbyville DE 19975

Call Sign: N3HFM
Dennis C Brady
64 Buntings Mill Ct
Selbyville DE 19975

Call Sign: N3HFN
Tina M Brady
64 Buntings Mill Ct
Selbyville DE 19975

Call Sign: WW4SCC
Southern Section Of The
Country Cousins
37816 Crab Bay Ln
Selbyville DE 19975

Call Sign: WA3ZRV
Frederick E Moreland
37816 Crab Bay Ln
Selbyville DE 199753924

Call Sign: WA2VZW
Brett J Halpin
36962 Creekhaven Dr
Selbyville DE 19975

Call Sign: WA2YYO
Deborah J Halpin
36962 Creekhaven Dr
Selbyville DE 19975

Call Sign: N6PRR
Susan Hensler
12 Dirickson Creek Rd
Selbyville DE 19975

Call Sign: K3RFF
Richard W Fleck
36834 Dupont Blvd
Selbyville DE 19975

Call Sign: W3WOV
William G Cook
36984 E Stoney Run
Selbyville DE 199754328

Call Sign: W3LOV
Thomas L Smith
37039 E Stoney Run
Selbyville DE 19975

Call Sign: KB3PT
William B Golden
59 E Tingle Dr
Selbyville DE 19975

Call Sign: W3LUV
William B Golden
59 E Tingle Dr
Selbyville DE 19975

Call Sign: KB3RAM
William Hamilton
39153 Garfield Ave
Selbyville DE 19975

Call Sign: KB3WZG
Frank W Hunt
38319 Maple Ln
Selbyville DE 19975

Call Sign: KA3SRB
Cornelius E Dominick Jr
5 Mill Pond Dr
Selbyville DE 199759530

Call Sign: KB3YCM
John D Enright
38250 Murphy Cir E
Selbyville DE 19975

Call Sign: KB3TVM
Del Mar Va Dx
Association
11 Princess Anne Ln
Selbyville DE 19975

Call Sign: W3PP
Del Mar Va Dx
Association
11 Princess Anne Ln
Selbyville DE 19975

Call Sign: K1RY
Roy G Gould
11 Princess Anne Ln
Selbyville DE 19975

Call Sign: KT3W
Del Mar Va Dx
Association
11 Princess Anne Ln
Selbyville DE 19975

Call Sign: KD3RY
Earl L Simpler
37223 Roxana Rd
Selbyville DE 19975

Call Sign: N3NPH
Ricky W Lewis
16 Ruth St
Selbyville DE 19975

Call Sign: KA3VLR
William Z Smith

73 Salty Way E
Selbyville DE 19975

Call Sign: N3UFA
Jack B Watson
37750 Salty Way W
Selbyville DE 19975

Call Sign: WA2PBR
Frank X Constantinople
36210 Sanderling Dr
Selbyville DE 19975

Call Sign: WA1WEJ
Laurent A Lynch
T & C Triler Park
Selbyville DE 19975

Call Sign: W3FIS
Paul W Ross
36951 Trout Terrace S
Selbyville DE 19975

Call Sign: WN3RGP
Carol A Spurrier
W Church St
Selbyville DE 19975

Call Sign: N3HMQ
Herman D Parsons Jr
Selbyville DE 19975

Call Sign: K3CNH
Harry C Spurrier
Selbyville DE 19975

Call Sign: WA3LNQ
Arthur I Rose
Selbyville DE 19975

Call Sign: W3TOP
Arthur I Rose
Selbyville DE 199750528

Call Sign: KB3UFO

Jonathan H Schafer
Selbyville DE 19975

FCC Amateur Radio License in Smyrna

Call Sign: N3ZIY
Edward J Taubert
154 Apoorva Ln
Smyrna DE 19977

Call Sign: KB3EMU
Mary B Carey
154 Apoorva Ln
Smyrna DE 19977

Call Sign: KE5NJ
Chris C Cote
342 Audrey Ln
Smyrna DE 19977

Call Sign: KB3RLK
Bernard J Matyniak Jr
1000 Big Oak Rd
Smyrna DE 19977

Call Sign: W3OWE
Bernard J Matyniak Jr
1000 Big Oak Rd
Smyrna DE 19977

Call Sign: K3CRK
Christopher R Kissell .
1474 Big Woods Rd
Smyrna DE 19977

Call Sign: KB3IGJ
Allen S Jester Jr
242 Black Diamond Rd
Smyrna DE 19977

Call Sign: K3CVZ
Ford J Powell
Box 68
Smyrna DE 19977

Call Sign: WA3ABK
Philip H Denney
Box 769
Smyrna DE 199779519

Call Sign: N3OMQ
Scott S Street
953 Boxwood Dr
Smyrna DE 19977

Call Sign: N3RPX
Rolland Cobia
90 Brian Dr Burtonwood
Village
Smyrna DE 19977

Call Sign: KB3NHK
Delaware Emergency
Management Agency
165 Brick Store Landing
Rd
Smyrna DE 19977

Call Sign: WD3EMA
Delaware Emergency
Management Agency
165 Brick Store Landing
Rd
Smyrna DE 19977

Call Sign: KB3ORL
Delaware State Police
165 Brickstore Landing Rd
Smyrna DE 19977

Call Sign: W3DSP
Delaware State Police
165 Brickstore Landing Rd
Smyrna DE 19977

Call Sign: WB3JUV
Grady C Ball
117 Brighton Pl
Smyrna DE 19977

Call Sign: WA3LYN
Troy G Sponaugle
23 Garrisons Cir
Smyrna DE 19977

Call Sign: KB3BJC
Charles C Vaughn
43 Hedgerow Hollow
Smyrna DE 19977

Call Sign: K8RUW
Bruce D Hulman
417 Kates Way
Smyrna DE 19977

Call Sign: K3OCE
Edward C Brown Jr
314 Lake Dr
Smyrna DE 19977

Call Sign: WA3BAO
Earl E Leasure Jr
432 Massey Church Rd
Smyrna DE 19977

Call Sign: W3BAO
Earl E Leasure Jr
432 Massey Church Rd
Smyrna DE 19977

Call Sign: KE6ZXA
June E Reames
135 N Main St
Smyrna DE 19977

Call Sign: KB3IYL
Jaclyn C Reames
135 N Main St
Smyrna DE 19977

Call Sign: KB3IYK
Jason R Reames
135 N Main St
Smyrna DE 19977

Call Sign: KB3LYP
John P Cereghin
38 S Carter Rd
Smyrna DE 19977

Call Sign: N3MES
Dean E Lubbers
253 Scott Ln
Smyrna DE 19977

Call Sign: KB3SLY
Barbara J Covert
219 Spring Meadow Dr
Smyrna DE 19977

Call Sign: KB3PRW
Douglas W Covert
219 Spring Meadow Dr
Smyrna DE 199774331

Call Sign: N3BBZ
Thomas S Leadbeater
56 Stanley Ave
Smyrna DE 19977

Call Sign: KD4CYJ
Charles R Lancaster
832 Stella St
Smyrna DE 199771797

Call Sign: WA3YXX
James R Hampton
764 Tush Rd
Smyrna DE 19977

Call Sign: KB3PCW
Darryl B Jones
207 W Commerce St
Smyrna DE 19977

Call Sign: N3QJJ
Kenneth R Steele
316 W Commerce St
Smyrna DE 19977

Call Sign: WB3ILR
Burton F Melvin Jr
85 W Cook Ave
Smyrna DE 19977

Call Sign: KB3VI
James M Baxter
35 W Glenwood Av Apt
7B
Smyrna DE 19977

Call Sign: N3QGW
Catherine A Simon
214 W Mt Vernon St
Smyrna DE 19977

Call Sign: KB3EGQ
Angelina P Hyland
422 W S St
Smyrna DE 19977

Call Sign: KB3EGP
Francis J Hyland
422 W S St
Smyrna DE 199771260

Call Sign: N4TEH
Taylor E Hoynes III
957 W South St
Smyrna DE 19977

Call Sign: KB3LUD
Taylor E Hoynes III
957 W South St
Smyrna DE 19977

Call Sign: KB3LUQ
Taylor E Hoynes III
957 W South St
Smyrna DE 19977

Call Sign: KB3HVP
Kevin K Richie
Smyrna DE 19977

FCC Amateur Radio License in South Bethany

Call Sign: W3PYY
Albert N Tomaso
89 Creek Rd Bayview Pk
South Bethany DE 19930

FCC Amateur Radio License in Stanton

Call Sign: KB3JAM
Sidney S Rice Jr
1111 Creekside Dr
Stanton DE 19804

FCC Amateur Radio License in Townsend

Call Sign: KC4JDT
Donald J Curry
699 Black Bird Station Rd
Townsend DE 19734

Call Sign: KB3OWZ
David W Young
445 Blackbird Landing Rd
Townsend DE 19734

Call Sign: W2EQZ
Marvin Goldstein
440 Caledonia Way
Townsend DE 19734

Call Sign: K3SXA
James J Friel
174 Deer Run Rd
Townsend DE 19734

Call Sign: KB3YCI
Byron C Anderson
249 Deer Run Rd
Townsend DE 19734

Call Sign: KA3IYO
Katherine Domanski
987 Dexter Corner Rd
Townsend DE 19734

Call Sign: WA3QPX
Paul J Domanski
987 Dexter Corner Rd
Townsend DE 19734

Call Sign: N3DLU
Warren T Crellin
1126 Dexter Corner Rd
Townsend DE 19734

Call Sign: AI3U
David R Agent
1069 Grears Corner Rd
Townsend DE 19734

Call Sign: N3XTK
Steven R Mackara
150 Logyard Ln
Townsend DE 19734

Call Sign: K3SRM
Steven R Mackara
150 Logyard Ln
Townsend DE 19734

Call Sign: N3TGN
Michael W Gardner
395 Maryland Line Rd
Townsend DE 19734

Call Sign: KB3OYP
Malcolm N Mcmullen
631 South St
Townsend DE 19734

Call Sign: W4LLH
Malcolm N Mcmullen
631 South St
Townsend DE 19734

Call Sign: KB3VLV
David C Driscall
617 Southerness Dr
Townsend DE 19734

Call Sign: WA3DCD
David C Driscall
617 Southerness Dr
Townsend DE 19734

Call Sign: N2KWN
James E Greene Jr
514 Stonehaven Dr
Townsend DE 19734

Call Sign: WB3DHO
James E Waecker Sr
5448 Summit Bridge Rd
Townsend DE 19734

Call Sign: N3TAQ
Uwe Davis
6058 Summit Bridge Rd
Townsend DE 19734

Call Sign: KB3MQF
Jay R Brackin
338 Union Church Rd
Townsend DE 197349109

Call Sign: W3NUR
Jay R Brackin
338 Union Church Rd
Townsend DE 197349109

Call Sign: N3YXT
William G Jopson
869 Union Church Rd
Townsend DE 19734

Call Sign: KB3QPF
Michael P Stradley
872 Union Church Rd
Townsend DE 19734

Call Sign: W3MPS
Michael P Stradley
872 Union Church Rd
Townsend DE 19734

Call Sign: KB3PTY
Paul R Christian
Townsend DE 19734

FCC Amateur Radio License in Viola

Call Sign: W2RPK
Clarence M Booz
400 Kersey Rd
Viola DE 19979

FCC Amateur Radio License in Wilmington

Call Sign: N3LOF
Frank W Langrell
24 2nd Ave
Wilmington DE 19808

Call Sign: N3QHE
William J Johnston Jr
203 3rd Ave
Wilmington DE 19804

Call Sign: N3KRC
Edward F Slawski
7 5th Ave
Wilmington DE 19805

Call Sign: KD4LS
Rodney A Johnson Jr
616 7th Ave
Wilmington DE 19808

Call Sign: W3QZI
Alonzo B Phillips
717 8th Ave
Wilmington DE 19808

Call Sign: KA3KGD
Donald E Hallam
2 Albany Pl
Wilmington DE
198051102

Call Sign: KB3GYA
John W Henderson Jr
23 Alcott Dr
Wilmington DE 19808

Call Sign: NE3G
Lawrence A Laravela
113 Allmond Ave
Wilmington DE 19803

Call Sign: KA3SMU
William L Melick
7 Alpine Ct
Wilmington DE 19810

Call Sign: KA3WSJ
Lillian P Ulmer
731 Ambleside Dr
Wilmington DE 19808

Call Sign: N3IAZ
Terence R Hunt
2806 Andys Ct
Wilmington DE 19810

Call Sign: NY3P
Richard M Valites
2114 Armour Dr
Wilmington DE 19808

Call Sign: N3JCK
John S Correale
1314 Arundel Dr
Wilmington DE 19808

Call Sign: N3LHW
George W Irwin
612 Augustine St

Wilmington DE
198042604

Call Sign: KB3PRV
Larry G Holderbaum
4619 Bailey Dr
Wilmington DE 19808

Call Sign: KA3LLL
James Hydzik
5611 Ball Rd
Wilmington DE 19808

Call Sign: K3QIO
James W Hydzik
5611 Ball Rd
Wilmington DE 19808

Call Sign: KA3TDS
William W Lenhard Jr
105 Balmore Ln
Wilmington DE 19808

Call Sign: KA3JUZ
John A Greblunas
13 Barbara Pl
Wilmington DE 19808

Call Sign: K3CNI
John W Chromy Jr
1122 Bardell Dr
Wilmington DE 19808

Call Sign: N3ADT
Charles F Killmon
2108 Barr Rd
Wilmington DE 19808

Call Sign: N3JJB
Terry J Lisansky
211 Barrett St
Wilmington DE 19802

Call Sign: KB3BBJ
Dmitry E Guskov

2316 Baynard Blvd
Wilmington DE 19802

Call Sign: KE3BY
William W Saunders
2316 Baynard Blvd
Wilmington DE 19802

Call Sign: N3QHB
Ugur Bekaroglu
2311 Beacon Hill Ln
Wilmington DE 19810

Call Sign: WA3TNP
Ira M Tartack
1812 Belfield Ave
Wilmington DE
198044006

Call Sign: KF4RGV
Sean O Clancy
1 Bell Hill Rd
Wilmington DE 19809

Call Sign: W3EOT
Richard W Sanford
100 Bellemoor St
Wilmington DE 19804

Call Sign: N3AYC
Arnold G Hanson
102 Belmont Ave
Wilmington DE 19804

Call Sign: W3LLL
Albert J Abramski
205 Belmont Ave
Wilmington DE 19804

Call Sign: N3VWH
Gerald N Vander Werff
119 Belmont Dr
Wilmington DE 19808

Call Sign: KA3QJN

William J Ryan Jr
726 Berry Rd
Wilmington DE 19810

Call Sign: KA3QJO
Gregory S Ryan
726 Berry Rd
Wilmington DE 19810

Call Sign: N3AYD
Judith Y Ryan
726 Berry Rd
Wilmington DE 19810

Call Sign: WB3DPJ
William J Ryan
726 Berry Rd
Wilmington DE 19810

Call Sign: K3UPY
William A Meekins Sr
12 Beverly Pl
Wilmington DE 19809

Call Sign: KB3PTP
John H Clark Jr
2139 Biddle St
Wilmington DE 19805

Call Sign: KA3AUG
Michael G Broujos
7 Binford Ln
Wilmington DE 19810

Call Sign: W3HKS
Frank J Valentine
609 Birmingham Ave
Wilmington DE 19804

Call Sign: WA3CPZ
Stoddard P Gray
2660 Bittersweet Dr The
Timbers
Wilmington DE
198101645

Call Sign: WA3ZYZ
Robert C Johnson
2526 Blackwood Rd
Wilmington DE
198103638

Call Sign: WA3NLU
Michael Foschini
2517 Bona Rd
Wilmington DE 19810

Call Sign: KA3SWW
Louis J Rombach
22 Boulder Brook Dr
Wilmington DE 19803

Call Sign: KA3KGG
Van D Olmstead Jr
Box 193
Wilmington DE 19899

Call Sign: KB3NCB
Dayspring School Amateur
Radio Club
10 Brackin Ave
Wilmington DE 19805

Call Sign: KB3NCC
Boy Scout Troop 30
Amateur Radio Club
10 Brackin Ave
Wilmington DE 19805

Call Sign: NR3I
Dayspring School Amateur
Radio Club
10 Brackin Ave
Wilmington DE
198052301

Call Sign: WB3LGC
Stephen M Shearer
10 Brackin Ave

Wilmington DE
198052301

Call Sign: KB3FMT
Renee M Shearer
10 Brackin Ave
Wilmington DE
198052301

Call Sign: KB3LUF
Andrew I Shearer
10 Brackin Ave
Wilmington DE 19805

Call Sign: KB3MEI
Robert M Shearer
10 Brackin Ave
Wilmington DE
198052301

Call Sign: KB3ELB
Stephen J Bell
15 Bradley Dr
Wilmington DE 19803

Call Sign: W3NX
Roy A Belair
415 Brighton Rd
Wilmington DE 19809

Call Sign: W3RDZ
Vernon L Turner Jr
606 Brighton Rd
Wilmington DE
198092825

Call Sign: KB3YDY
Jason P Graham
10 Britton Pl
Wilmington DE 19805

Call Sign: WA3WUL
Bruce D Crawford
5 Broadbent Rd
Wilmington DE 19810

Call Sign: N3EQW
Doris F Whisler
3602 Brookfield Ave
Wilmington DE 19803

Call Sign: W3LEU
George E Whisler
3602 Brookfield Ave
Wilmington DE 19803

Call Sign: KB3SUM
Craig A Skotnicki
209 Brookland Ave
Wilmington DE 19805

Call Sign: W3FME
Ralph W Churchill
1902 Brookside Ln
Wilmington DE 19803

Call Sign: KB3GNJ
Keith F Churchill
1902 Brookside Ln
Wilmington DE
198033510

Call Sign: KB3GNK
Marilyn E Churchill
1902 Brookside Ln
Wilmington DE
198033510

Call Sign: KA3SMZ
Andrew K Williams
2114 Buckingham Rd
Wilmington DE 19810

Call Sign: W3WJM
William J Martin
719 Burnley Rd
Wilmington DE 19803

Call Sign: N3HRJ
George E Kirvan Jr

2421 Calf Run Dr
Wilmington DE 19808

Call Sign: AF3I
Harold A Mc Caffrey
500 Calhoun Rd
Wilmington DE 19809

Call Sign: KC3RF
Michael R Short
114 Canterbury Dr
Wilmington DE
198032608

Call Sign: KB3RLO
Jim R Upson
3212 Cardiff Dr
Wilmington DE 19810

Call Sign: K3JRU
Jim R Upson
3212 Cardiff Dr
Wilmington DE 19810

Call Sign: KB3HMQ
Richard K Parker
2200 Carlton Ln
Wilmington DE 19810

Call Sign: KA8UWA
Mike B Keesey
1989 Carol Dr
Wilmington DE 19808

Call Sign: N3EGR
Derick W Ovenall
1209 Carr Rd
Wilmington DE 19809

Call Sign: KB3RLJ
R Brian Crozier
9 Catalpa Ave
Wilmington DE 19804

Call Sign: N3RHP

Shawn A Rudd
4904 Catamaran Ct
Wilmington DE 19808

Call Sign: K3HXA
Robert E Wolstenholme
2411 Cedar Ave
Wilmington DE 19808

Call Sign: AB3DE
Richard J Hampson
2517 Cedar Tree Dr Apt
3B
Wilmington DE 19810

Call Sign: WA3VQA
Andrew Bruce
901 Centerville Rd
Wilmington DE 19804

Call Sign: N3AQX
Howard W Swank
3700 Centerville Rd
Wilmington DE 19807

Call Sign: N3TXQ
Paul C Griffith
2801 Centre Rd
Wilmington DE 19805

Call Sign: N3PTB
Joseph I Larson
403 Champlain Ave
Wilmington DE 19804

Call Sign: K3FDE
Herbert M Diehl
1706 Cherry St
Wilmington DE 19809

Call Sign: K3EWP
Joseph B Dale
1 Chestnut Ave
Wilmington DE
198055424

Call Sign: KA3MNJ
Gerald R Schocie
307 Chestnut Ave
Wilmington DE
198093225

Call Sign: N3GLS
Michael D Keown
119 Chestnut Ave Apt C-4
Wilmington DE
198055435

Call Sign: N3RQI
David L Benfer
11 Chilton Rd
Wilmington DE 19803

Call Sign: W6AAB
Alexander Maromaty
115 Christina Landing Dr
Apt 709
Wilmington DE 19801

Call Sign: N3JWL
Denise P Gilmore
2510 Cinder Rd
Wilmington DE 19810

Call Sign: W3GQP
Warren F Guss Jr
2510 Cinder Rd
Wilmington DE 19810

Call Sign: N3ZOO
Thomas J Burton
4605 Claremont Ct
Wilmington DE 19808

Call Sign: KB3TCZ
Dennis J Perrone Jr
3410 Clayton Ave
Wilmington DE 19808

Call Sign: AA3FM

Ralph B Poole
1524 Cleland Course
Wilmington DE 19805

Call Sign: K3LFC
Frank R Caruso IV
1310 Clifford Rd
Wilmington DE 19805

Call Sign: N3MDY
James R Ward
42 Colefax Ct
Wilmington DE
198042950

Call Sign: KA3ZTU
Randolph M Allen
4103 Coleridge Rd
Wilmington DE
198021907

Call Sign: KB3PLE
Jay N Goldman
2207 Concord Pike 533
Wilmington DE
198032908

Call Sign: K3OBI
Jay N Goldman
2207 Concord Pike 533
Wilmington DE
198032908

Call Sign: KB3VEO
David M Christian
100 Congresional Dr Apt
B
Wilmington DE 19807

Call Sign: N3AHB
James K Durborow
211 Cordon Rd
Wilmington DE 19803

Call Sign: WA3LNX

Walter Domorod
18 Cornell Rd
Wilmington DE 19808

Call Sign: K3NFL
William R Goodman
308 Cornwall Rd
Wilmington DE 19803

Call Sign: N3EDB
Edward J Starr
309 Corval Pl
Wilmington DE
198041124

Call Sign: KB3IBM
Oliver V Suddard
503 Country Club Dr
Wilmington DE 19803

Call Sign: K1HDT
Hector D Trestini
1092 Creekside Dr
Wilmington DE 19804

Call Sign: KB2RCB
Michael F Grusell
1261 Creekside Dr
Wilmington DE 19804

Call Sign: K3BES
Robert J Schwarz
5441 Crestline Rd
Wilmington DE 19808

Call Sign: K3DTX
Melvin Bedford
3309 Cross Country Dr
Greenview
Wilmington DE 19810

Call Sign: N3JCJ
Fred F Butzi
1102 Dardel Dr
Wilmington DE 19803

Call Sign: N3CUT
Samuel C Winram
2506 Deepwood Dr
Wilmington DE 19810

Call Sign: KD1IJ
Kent E Gabrys
32 Degas Cir
Wilmington DE 19808

Call Sign: N3UCL
Arthur E Vincent
2109 Delaview Ave
Wilmington DE 19810

Call Sign: KA3KHZ
Douglas E Rambo
105 Delaware Ave
Wilmington DE 19803

Call Sign: WA9GOV
Gary E Hindes
1400 Delaware Ave
Wilmington DE 19806

Call Sign: N3IIH
Katherine M Day
1508 Delwood Rd
Wilmington DE 19803

Call Sign: K3VWQ
Nathan H Weissman
9 Devon Ct
Wilmington DE 19810

Call Sign: KB3VFJ
Richard B Hays
144 Devonshire Rd
Wilmington DE 19803

Call Sign: KB3PTO
James D Allison
2415 Donlon Rd
Wilmington DE 19803

Call Sign: W3GQL
Harry B Francisco
2703 Doris Dr
Wilmington DE
198032525

Call Sign: N3ENI
Bart Di Carlo
2505 Dorval Rd
Wilmington DE 19810

Call Sign: KB3ALP
Aaron M Tarpine
10 Drummond Dr
Wilmington DE 19808

Call Sign: KB3UBG
John L Proctor
20 Duvall Ct
Wilmington DE
198082143

Call Sign: N3ZIK
Jose E Abraham
809 E 17th St
Wilmington DE 19802

Call Sign: N3EYW
Lemuel R James
535 E 35th St
Wilmington DE
198022817

Call Sign: KE4ERF
Joshua E Gates
5 E Brookland Ave
Wilmington DE 19805

Call Sign: KB3VKZ
James W Domorod Sr
1101 E Newport Pike
Wilmington DE
198041922

Call Sign: W1AKG
James W Domorod Sr
1101 E Newport Pike
Wilmington DE
198041922

Call Sign: KE3ZU
Alfred G Le Sieur
2724 E Riding Dr
Wilmington DE 19808

Call Sign: W3AHW
Royden E Hager
2618 E Robino Dr
Wilmington DE 19808

Call Sign: KB2VXM
William E Neide Jr
6 E Salisbury Dr
Wilmington DE 19809

Call Sign: N3TRM
William F Owens
8 E Sumimit Ave
Wilmington DE 19804

Call Sign: N3AYA
Rodger A Nelson Dr
211 East Ct
Wilmington DE 19810

Call Sign: W3DRA
Delaware Repeater
Association
2711 Ebright Rd
Wilmington DE 19810

Call Sign: W2NCN
William H Greenhalgh
2711 Ebright Rd
Wilmington DE
198101128

Call Sign: W3DE
William H Greenhalgh

2711 Ebright Rd
Wilmington DE
198101128

Call Sign: K3NEF
Benjamin L Blake Jr
92 Echo Rd
Wilmington DE 19810

Call Sign: N3AEG
D Eckel Sr
1219 Elderon Dr
Wilmington DE
198081909

Call Sign: N3UXS
James J Hynes
2319 Empire Dr
Wilmington DE 19810

Call Sign: KB3VYI
Max Haggerty
706 Euclid Ave
Wilmington DE 19809

Call Sign: N3DEF
Edward F Harrison
3887 Evelyn Dr
Wilmington DE 19808

Call Sign: KA3YAQ
Alexander P Mc Cann
2002 Fairwood Ln
Wilmington DE 19810

Call Sign: K3ZKA
John H Taylor
5 Falcon Ct
Wilmington DE 19808

Call Sign: KB3NFF
Johnnie R Meadows
22 Falcon Ct
Wilmington DE 19808

Call Sign: K3JRM
Johnnie R Meadows
22 Falcon Ct
Wilmington DE 19808

Call Sign: N4POV
Peter Zazzi
3205 Falcon Ln 313
Wilmington DE 19808

Call Sign: K3PEH
Patrick E Hennessy
503 Farwell Rd
Wilmington DE 19804

Call Sign: KA3UAU
Douglas J Griest
2306 Faulkland Rd
Wilmington DE 19805

Call Sign: KS3E
John M Lanyon Jr
2806 Fawkes Dr
Wilmington DE 19808

Call Sign: KB3YLH
Melissa J Patro
214 Fenwick Ave
Wilmington DE 19804

Call Sign: N3DQH
Willard E Warrington
235 Fenwick Ave
Wilmington DE 19804

Call Sign: KA3OSI
Robert O Wardell
1102 Flint Hill Rd Arundel
Wilmington DE
198081912

Call Sign: KA3MZX
Jeffrey H Shoemaker
107 Florence Ave
Wilmington DE 19803

Call Sign: KB3JCB
Jeffrey Bradshaw
120 Florence Ave
Wilmington DE 19803

Call Sign: KD0GV
Larry J Van Stone
228 Florence Ave
Wilmington DE
198032340

Call Sign: NC3M
Kenneth C Pierce Sr
311 Forest Dr
Wilmington DE 19804

Call Sign: N3LUD
John G Di Giovanni
1448 Forsythia Ave
Wilmington DE 19810

Call Sign: W3HIH
Martin Gibbs
2300 Foster Pl
Wilmington DE 19806

Call Sign: N3JMV
David J Holmes
500 Foulk Rd
Wilmington DE 19803

Call Sign: KA3BTW
Shanmuga S Jayakumar
600 Foulk Rd
Wilmington DE 19803

Call Sign: N3LOG
Mark L Meldon
400 Foulk Rd Apt 4B8
Wilmington DE 19803

Call Sign: KB3RUX
Edward J Stahl Jr
2604 Frederick Ave

Wilmington DE 19805

Call Sign: KB3WFP
Owen D Hughes
1421 Fresno Rd
Wilmington DE 19803

Call Sign: KB3RLN
Graeme L Baker
1435 Fresno Rd
Wilmington DE 19803

Call Sign: N3QBF
Raymond M Sokola
416 Garland Rd
Wilmington DE 19803

Call Sign: N3MEQ
David M Kufta
26 Georgetown Ave
Wilmington DE
198091250

Call Sign: K3SJR
Leo B Hogan Jr
1021 Gilpin Ave
Wilmington DE 19806

Call Sign: N3XNM
Winfield J Heckert
134 Glenoak Rd
Wilmington DE 19805

Call Sign: KA3TKR
Ricky J Crossan
10 Glenway Pl
Wilmington DE 19804

Call Sign: AB3IB
Jared C Smith
5423 Golf View Dr Apt
A2
Wilmington DE 19808

Call Sign: N3LGJ

Marvin D Forman
2403 Granby Rd
Wilmington DE 19810

Call Sign: KA3CZK
John Glenn Jr
12 Granite Rd
Wilmington DE 19803

Call Sign: N3KPQ
Joseph B Ruggiero
2100 Grayling Ct
Wilmington DE 19804

Call Sign: K3MPZ
Ralph L Hairsine
709 Greenbank Rd
Wilmington DE
198083167

Call Sign: KA3ZNA
Deanna M Parker
125 Greenbank Rd D 11
Wilmington DE 19808

Call Sign: KB3SLW
Carol I Buswell
2413 Greenleaf Dr
Wilmington DE 19810

Call Sign: N3RHQ
Walter A Lumley
447 Greenwood Dr
Wilmington DE 19808

Call Sign: KB3QVE
Theodore F Bond
481 Greenwood Dr
Wilmington DE 19808

Call Sign: WA3AVV
Charles H Arrington
711 Greenwood Rd
Wilmington DE 19801

Call Sign: WV3O
Joseph W Kremer
19 Gristmill Ct
Wilmington DE 19803

Call Sign: KA3VWL
Emily M Ferrara
1705 Gunning Dr
Wilmington DE 19803

Call Sign: KA3WSV
Richard B Ferrara
1705 Gunning Dr
Wilmington DE 19803

Call Sign: WG3D
Louis B Ferrara
1705 Gunning Dr
Wilmington DE 19803

Call Sign: W4RHR
Ronald H Rust
14 Guyencourt Rd
Wilmington DE 19807

Call Sign: KB3LTK
W3Nx Memorial Station
1005 Haines Ave
Wilmington DE 19809

Call Sign: W3NX
W3Nx Memorial Station
1005 Haines Ave
Wilmington DE 19809

Call Sign: KB3EHU
Arthur L Hitchens
1005 Haines Ave
Wilmington DE 19809

Call Sign: N3DXX
Arthur L Hitchens
1005 Haines Ave
Wilmington DE 19809

Call Sign: N2WPZ
Joel A Harrison
1224 Haines Ave
Wilmington DE 19809

Call Sign: N3HVD
Robert S Mullins
620 Halstead Rd
Wilmington DE 19803

Call Sign: W3DEP
Charles D Mc Kinney Jr
705 Halstead Rd
Wilmington DE 19803

Call Sign: KB3GNH
Kevin Adams
2411 Hammond Pl
Wilmington DE
198084208

Call Sign: N3APA
Arthur W Fynsk
316 Hampton Rd
Wilmington DE 19803

Call Sign: N3DNG
Jorgen J Hansen
1 Hancock Pl
Wilmington DE 19806

Call Sign: KD3OJ
Edward J Parker
511 Hanover Rd
Wilmington DE 19809

Call Sign: KB3UGO
Jeffrey S Tversky
100 Harding Ave
Wilmington DE 19804

Call Sign: N3SXO
Nicholas V Rhoads
111 Harding Ave
Wilmington DE 19804

Call Sign: N3RSD
Jesse F Hickam Jr
25 Harlech Dr
Wilmington DE 19807

Call Sign: W3HDC
Kenneth C Bass Jr
29 Harlech Dr Anglesey
Wilmington DE 19807

Call Sign: KB3PZP
William A Durnan
4 Harrington Ct
Wilmington DE
198051867

Call Sign: N3SKM
Colman L Hipkins
29 Harvard
Wilmington DE 19808

Call Sign: WA3QQW
George Hassell
27 Harvard Rd
Wilmington DE 19808

Call Sign: N3SXP
Stephen Hryckewycz II
825 Harwood Rd
Wilmington DE 19804

Call Sign: N3ZHB
Millard H Widdekind
829 Harwood Rd
Wilmington DE
198042662

Call Sign: KQ4QR
Jerry L Goldman
2018 Harwyn Rd
Wilmington DE 19810

Call Sign: W3MAX
Jerry L Goldman

2018 Harwyn Rd
Wilmington DE 19810

Call Sign: N3SUW
Peter W Guilday
2218 Hearn Rd
Wilmington DE 19803

Call Sign: KB3MGT
David T Garland
7 Henry Ct
Wilmington DE 19808

Call Sign: N3EU
John S Mc Daniel
3305 Heritage Dr
Wilmington DE
198081522

Call Sign: KB3VSR
Robert P Lutz
3324 Hermitage Rd
Wilmington DE 19810

Call Sign: KA7RDN
James Q Townley
3601 Hewn Ln 542
Wilmington DE
198051732

Call Sign: KB3NYD
Jason Parrott
4 Hidden Oaks Blvd
Wilmington DE 19808

Call Sign: KB3OJI
Walter Clifton
1101 Highland Ave
Marshalton Hgts
Wilmington DE
198045813

Call Sign: WA3DBL
Kent W Farlow
1109 Hillside Ave

Wilmington DE 19809

Call Sign: N3ZRV
Richard E Verbanc
1220 Hillside Blvd
Wilmington DE
198034212

Call Sign: KA3SNB
Wendy L Friz
115 Hitching Post Dr
Wilmington DE 19803

Call Sign: KB3EFY
Walter R Williamson
123 Hitching Post Dr
Wilmington DE 19803

Call Sign: W3TRC
William A Zehner
111 Hoiland Dr
Wilmington DE 19803

Call Sign: WA3MRX
Wayne C Anglero
201 Hoiland Dr Shipley
Hts
Wilmington DE
198033229

Call Sign: N3JJC
Robert J Everett
17 Holly Hill Rd
Wilmington DE 19809

Call Sign: W3XT
John J Keegan Jr
26 Holly Ln
Wilmington DE 19807

Call Sign: WB3JTK
Frederick T Forkner
19 Homewood Rd
Wilmington DE 19803

Call Sign: KB3MJZ
Peter Jernakoff
3527 Hopkins Dr
Wilmington DE 19808

Call Sign: K3KMS
Peter Jernakoff
3527 Hopkins Dr
Wilmington DE 19808

Call Sign: W3EKO
Jean M Adams
2404 Horace Dr
Wilmington DE 19808

Call Sign: KA0JDW
Richard W Lewis
2221 Inwood Rd
Wilmington DE 19810

Call Sign: N3IOI
Mary T Lewis
2221 Inwood Rd
Wilmington DE 19810

Call Sign: KA3BLW
Edgar A Boys
2403 Ivanhoe Ln
Wilmington DE 19808

Call Sign: KB3SUT
Joseph L Olivere
2516 Jacqueline Dr C-33
Wilmington DE 19810

Call Sign: KB7TFF
Melissa N Donimirski
2520 Jacqueline Dr D-24
Wilmington DE 19810

Call Sign: N3DLM
Guerrino J Mascelli Jr
119 Jade Dr
Wilmington DE 19810

Call Sign: N3OVE
Jay H Smith
2321 Jamaica Dr
Wilmington DE 19810

Call Sign: WF0J
Victoria J Smith
2321 Jamaica Dr
Wilmington DE 19810

Call Sign: WA2GIC
Paul V Sproul
1402 Jan Dr
Wilmington DE 19803

Call Sign: N3FVR
Frank J Lukens
1008 Jeffrey Rd
Wilmington DE 19810

Call Sign: KA3OQZ
David M Connors
2333 Katherine
Wilmington DE 19808

Call Sign: W4PZ
Donald E Shaffer
5921 Kennett Pike
Wilmington DE 19807

Call Sign: KB3JAK
Timothy D Swanson
109 Kennwood Ln
Wilmington DE
198042348

Call Sign: KB3JIF
Kevin C Welch
1004 Kent Rd
Wilmington DE 19807

Call Sign: KB3MCO
James E Fletcher
1327 Kenwood Rd
Wilmington DE 19805

Call Sign: WA3EJT
James E Fletcher
1327 Kenwood Rd
Wilmington DE 19805

Call Sign: KA3MNI
Paul E Sweeney
1952 Lakeview Rd
Wilmington DE 19805

Call Sign: N3BUK
Robert J Morgan
1969 Lakeview Rd
Wilmington DE 19805

Call Sign: N3CRV
Benjamin H Poles Sr
1106 Lakewood Dr
Wilmington DE
198033506

Call Sign: W3BEN
Benjamin H Poles Sr
1106 Lakewood Dr
Wilmington DE
198033506

Call Sign: KB3AJS
Michael G Mixon
2211 Lancashire Dr
Wilmington DE 19810

Call Sign: KB3VHD
Michael I Brumberger
137 Landis Way N
Wilmington DE 19803

Call Sign: WB3DEL
Michael I Brumberger
137 Landis Way N
Wilmington DE 19803

Call Sign: WB2YAT
Michael S Ruderman

2706 Landon Dr
Wilmington DE 19810

Call Sign: K3LVS
Alfred A Brizzolara Jr
2712 Landsdowne Dr
Cardiff
Wilmington DE 19810

Call Sign: KB3MLT
John R Orr
201 Laurel Ave
Wilmington DE 19809

Call Sign: KB3IEM
Frederick R Cullis
8 Laurel Ct
Wilmington DE 19808

Call Sign: AC3R
Richard W York
410 Lee Ter
Wilmington DE
198031813

Call Sign: N3RHK
Thomas M Butler
412 Lee Ter
Wilmington DE 19803

Call Sign: K3BYA
Kern M Bowyer
16 Lehigh Ave
Wilmington DE 19805

Call Sign: KA3WOK
Robert W Gooden
1809 Limestone Rd
Wilmington DE 19804

Call Sign: KB3VOF
Grace Mcconkie
4701 Limestone Rd
Wilmington DE 19808

Call Sign: KB3PTZ
James B Mcconkie
4701 Limestone Rd
Wilmington DE 19808

Call Sign: KB3RKE
Robert T Mcconkie
4701 Limestone Rd 2A1
Wilmington DE 19808

Call Sign: KB3TPB
New Castle County
Communication Corp
107 Lincoln Ave
Wilmington DE 19804

Call Sign: K3NCC
New Castle County
Communication Corps
107 Lincoln Ave
Wilmington DE 19804

Call Sign: KB3UWY
Erik Eisenman
2503 Lindell Rd
Wilmington DE 19808

Call Sign: KA3SMT
Felix R Santiago
4 Littlewood Ln
Wilmington DE 19807

Call Sign: K3ONO
William C Blatz
3 Lloyd Cir Weber Tract
Wilmington DE
198101324

Call Sign: KB3BER
Albert F Rose Sr
2630 Longfellow Dr
Wilmington DE 19808

Call Sign: KB3GEO
Anthony J Graziano

2647 Longwood Dr
Wilmington DE 19810

Call Sign: WA3WCE
Robert H Rothenmeyer
710 Loper Ln
Wilmington DE 19808

Call Sign: KC3ZA
Philip B Fuhrman
714 Lore Ave
Wilmington DE 19809

Call Sign: N3ZAO
Joseph A Bradshaw
3109 Loudoun Dr
Wilmington DE 19808

Call Sign: N3ZJT
Cassandra L Bradshaw
3109 Loudoun Dr
Wilmington DE 19808

Call Sign: K3ARM
Charles L Maxwell Sr
2011 Lynch Dr
Wilmington DE
198084822

Call Sign: KA3RUN
Cynthia M Monaco
68 Lynthwaite Farm Ln
Wilmington DE 19803

Call Sign: KA3WOL
John J Mullarkey
13 Madelyn Ave
Wilmington DE 19803

Call Sign: N3DYC
Howard G Shoemaker
2402 Magnolia Dr
Wilmington DE 19810

Call Sign: KB3VAY

Harold Clemens
500 Maple Ave
Wilmington DE 19809

Call Sign: N3DND
Hardy W Wilbank Sr
107 Maple Ave
Wilmington DE 19809

Call Sign: N3DXV
Judy A Wilbank
107 Maple Ave
Wilmington DE 19809

Call Sign: KB3UCV
Steven Fisher
1903 Maple St
Wilmington DE 19805

Call Sign: W3AQ
John J Turner
2613 Marhill Dr
Wilmington DE 19810

Call Sign: K3CIU
David M Morales
1 Marker Dr
Wilmington DE
198102260

Call Sign: WV8PC
Paul J Cutright
322 Marsh Rd
Wilmington DE 19809

Call Sign: KB3GEN
Courtney Moore
1612 Marsh Rod
Wilmington DE 19803

Call Sign: N3ETJ
Paul O Knight
403 Marshfield Rd
Wilmington DE 19803

Call Sign: N3ZJV
Alan E Start Jr
40 Marta Dr
Wilmington DE 19808

Call Sign: WB3HYW
Linda M Mc Elhone
51 Marta Dr
Wilmington DE 19808

Call Sign: WB3IKK
Thomas W Mc Elhone
51 Marta Dr
Wilmington DE 19808

Call Sign: WB3ENE
Elliott P Smith
2908 Mattahoon Rd
Wilmington DE 19808

Call Sign: KB3JGV
Terrance M Clark
101 Matthes Pl
Wilmington DE 19804

Call Sign: KA3VZD
Thomas R Ownsby
2150 Melson Rd Apt B21
Wilmington DE 19808

Call Sign: KC3KZ
Sholom Kass
1900 Millers Rd
Wilmington DE 19810

Call Sign: W3AFB
Francis W Weldin
404 Milltown Rd
Wilmington DE 19808

Call Sign: WR7I
Mark S Mallett
1111 Milltown Rd
Wilmington DE
198083001

Call Sign: KA3OIJ
John E Kern
1606 Milltown Rd
Wilmington DE 19808

Call Sign: WP2AHE
Joseph L Despins
120 Monet Cir
Wilmington DE
198081120

Call Sign: KB3DIZ
Eric D Boehm
1011 Montgomery Rd
Wilmington DE 19805

Call Sign: N3OMW
Vincent A Boehm Jr
1011 Montgomery Rd
Wilmington DE 19805

Call Sign: KB3UWZ
Patrick E Hennessy
1209 Montgomery Rd
Wilmington DE 19805

Call Sign: N4RLC
David C Herrell II
9 Morgan Ln
Wilmington DE 19808

Call Sign: KB3NFG
John S Bradford
725 Mount Lebanon Rd
Wilmington DE 19803

Call Sign: N3XYI
Peter R Parlett
1206 Mullet Rd
Wilmington DE 19808

Call Sign: W3GAU
Joseph L Gillson
109 Mullin Rd

Wilmington DE 19809

Call Sign: N3HDR
Carl W Thompson III
902 N Adams St
Wilmington DE 19801

Call Sign: KB3GEL
Jason J Snead
27 N Cannon Dr
Wilmington DE 19809

Call Sign: KA2HKV
Stephen E Byrnes
1420 N Clayton St
Wilmington DE
198064082

Call Sign: N3ZIJ
Manuel Gonzalez
221 N Connell St
Wilmington DE 19805

Call Sign: N3ZIG
Agapito Jimenez
223 N Connell St
Wilmington DE 19805

Call Sign: KB3RLG
Frank R Caruso IV
909 N Dupont Rd
Wilmington DE 19807

Call Sign: N3JAB
Juan Martinez
401 N Harrison St
Wilmington DE 19805

Call Sign: N3QHI
Maria M Rodriguez
401 N Harrison St
Wilmington DE 19805

Call Sign: KA3VAN
Carolyn M Lane

2920 N Harrison St
Wilmington DE 19802

Call Sign: KD7BPI
Peter A Brown
1300 N Harrison St Apt
A401
Wilmington DE 19806

Call Sign: AD3M
Frank T Filipkowski Jr
1130 N Hilton Rd
Wilmington DE 19803

Call Sign: KB3QCU
Marek Wrobel
107 N Lincoln St
Wilmington DE 19805

Call Sign: KB3PTM
Joseph J Farnan III
919 N Market St 12th
Floor
Wilmington DE 19801

Call Sign: KA3TZH
Gregory D Jones
1113 N Overhill Ct
Wilmington DE 19810

Call Sign: KB3MIX
Brent D Frye
610 N Tatnall St Apt 2F
Wilmington DE 19801

Call Sign: KB9NUX
Michael J Kiefer
5046 N Tupelo Turn
Wilmington DE
198081024

Call Sign: KB3QKF
Michael J Kiefer
5046 N Tupelo Turn

Wilmington DE
198081024

Call Sign: KB3FLZ
Jay G Lantz
2605 Naamans Rd
Wilmington DE 19810

Call Sign: W3PQ
David R Elzey
5102 New Kent Rd
Wilmington DE
198082706

Call Sign: N3PCK
Wayne A Ritchie
1305 New St
Wilmington DE 19808

Call Sign: NC3S
Philip G Marsh
2828 Newport Gap Pike
Wilmington DE 19808

Call Sign: WA3NSS
Joseph E Garber
2904 Newport Gap Pike
Wilmington DE 19808

Call Sign: KB3VKY
Kurt C Bryson
3805 Newport Gap Pike
Wilmington DE 19808

Call Sign: K3WPD
Kurt C Bryson
3805 Newport Gap Pike
Wilmington DE 19808

Call Sign: WB3GSN
Kurt C Bryson
3805 Newport Gap Pike
Wilmington DE 19808

Call Sign: KB3YCJ

Corey D Buterbaugh
2500 Nicholby Dr
Wilmington DE 19808

Call Sign: N3MEB
David W Mackenzie
415 Nichols Ave
Wilmington DE 19803

Call Sign: KA3CCZ
Anton W Benson
3704 Oak Ridge Rd
Wilmington DE
198081339

Call Sign: KA3FKC
Le Roy F Meredith
212 Oakwood Rd
Wilmington DE 19803

Call Sign: KA3WKQ
Ben Z Tolpin
1309 Oberlin Rd
Wilmington DE 19803

Call Sign: WA3V
Eugene I Tolpin
1309 Oberlin Rd
Wilmington DE 19803

Call Sign: N3ZXJ
James Wilkins III
205 Odessa Ave
Wilmington DE 19809

Call Sign: KB3LYN
Robert M Gerber
4806 Old Capital Trail
Wilmington DE 19808

Call Sign: KA3TKQ
Maryann M Crossan
4817 Old Capitol Trl Apt
116
Wilmington DE 19808

Call Sign: KA3IXF
William J Parker Jr
3314 Old Capitol Trl K-12
Wilmington DE 19808

Call Sign: K3WHU
William L Michelinie
127 Oldbury Dr
Wilmington DE 19808

Call Sign: KB3PTQ
Steven D Rinehart
163 Oldbury Dr
Wilmington DE 19808

Call Sign: W3URR
George A Moyer Jr
11 Orchard Ln
Wilmington DE 19809

Call Sign: KD3VD
A James Laurino
2207 Orleans Rd
Wilmington DE 19810

Call Sign: KB3SQG
John W Dolan
200 Owls Nest Rd
Wilmington DE 19807

Call Sign: K3JWD
John W Dolan
200 Owls Nest Rd
Wilmington DE 19807

Call Sign: W3LH
John W Dolan
200 Owls Nest Rd
Wilmington DE 19807

Call Sign: KB3VQU
Clifford R Marks
209 Paddock Ln
Wilmington DE 19803

Call Sign: KB3TGI
Joshua A Marks
209 Paddock Ln
Wilmington DE 19803

Call Sign: N3ACU
John D Thompson
17 Paisley Dr
Wilmington DE 19808

Call Sign: KY3G
Michael K Athey
49 Paladin Club
Wilmington DE 19802

Call Sign: N3MKU
Loren E Leach
100 Paladin Dr
Wilmington DE 19802

Call Sign: KA3SNA
Karen A Mc Kinstry
2 Palomino Ct
Wilmington DE 19803

Call Sign: KB3QQZ
Cornelia N Winner
1704 Park Dr Unit 208
Wilmington DE 19806

Call Sign: WA3I
Chester A Thayer II
123 Parrish Ln
Wilmington DE
198103457

Call Sign: WA3AAY
Maurice T Black
55 Paschall Rd
Wilmington DE 19803

Call Sign: KB3NTH
Carl Krauthauser
2308 Patwynn Rd

Wilmington DE 19810

Call Sign: K3NTH
Carl Krauthauser
2308 Patwynn Rd
Wilmington DE 19810

Call Sign: NT3H
Carl Krauthauser
2308 Patwynn Rd
Wilmington DE 19810

Call Sign: W3EGN
O Lloyd Shorter Jr
6 Penarth Dr
Wilmington DE 19803

Call Sign: KA3GNS
Louis H Jackson
26 Penarth Dr
Wilmington DE 19803

Call Sign: K3FO
Coy Waddell
1716 Penguin Rd
Wilmington DE 19809

Call Sign: K3BPQ
Joseph P Budd
4816 Pennington Ct
Wilmington DE 19808

Call Sign: KA3UYM
Donald R Morrison
2627 Pennington Dr
Wilmington DE 19810

Call Sign: K3ZQD
Nicholas P Bash
2401 Pennsylvania Ave
Wilmington DE 19806

Call Sign: KB3QCX
Thomas R Macom
5209 Perry Pl

Wilmington DE 19810

Call Sign: KB3LIA
William R Bushey
18 Perth Dr
Wilmington DE 19803

Call Sign: AB3CB
William R Bushey
18 Perth Dr
Wilmington DE 19803

Call Sign: K3EK
William R Bushey
18 Perth Dr
Wilmington DE 19803

Call Sign: WB3EXW
James J Messick
2710 Pickering Rd
Wilmington DE 19808

Call Sign: WB3KEP
Keith T Reynolds
4602 Pickwick Dr
Wilmington DE 19808

Call Sign: W3OHD
Howard F Weldin
243 Pinehurst Rd
Wilmington DE 19803

Call Sign: KA3VNY
David C Floyd
6 Plover Ct
Wilmington DE 19808

Call Sign: KA3UJO
Richard E Gallaher Jr
1444 Propect Dr
Wilmington DE 19809

Call Sign: KB3HAA
Augustus H Clagett III
426 Prospect Ave

Wilmington DE 19803

Call Sign: KB3QVC
William M Quinn
428 Prospect Ave
Wilmington DE 19803

Call Sign: K3QVC
William M Quinn
428 Prospect Ave
Wilmington DE 19803

Call Sign: WN3J
Charles E Tubbs
1976 Prospect Rd
Wilmington DE 19805

Call Sign: KE4PS
Robert A Chuda
321 Quimby Dr
Wilmington DE
198083615

Call Sign: KB3CER
William W Zeitler
1307 Quincy Dr
Wilmington DE 19803

Call Sign: AB3GD
John D Griffin Jr
2415 Rambler Rd
Wilmington DE 19810

Call Sign: WA3THL
Robert D Morris
22 Ramblewood Dr
Wilmington DE 19810

Call Sign: K3NI
Clark W Heckert
16 Ravine Rd
Wilmington DE 19810

Call Sign: KB3UDU
Pamela B Heckert

16 Ravine Rd
Wilmington DE 19810

Call Sign: KB3VSS
Peter B Heckert
16 Ravine Rd
Wilmington DE 19810

Call Sign: W3VE
David L Mc Guigan
515 Riblett Ln
Wilmington DE 19808

Call Sign: KB3UWX
Van D Olmstead
10 Richards Dr
Wilmington DE
198103901

Call Sign: KD5AKP
Paul E Morgan
7 Rockford Rd C14
Wilmington DE 19806

Call Sign: N3WBF
Douglas G Batt
117 Rockingham Dr
Wilmington DE 19803

Call Sign: W3ANI
Charles P De Neef Sr
1519 Rockland Rd Apt 334
Wilmington DE 19803

Call Sign: KA3RFP
Barbara K Eisenman
503 Rockwood Rd
Wilmington DE 19802

Call Sign: K3KSH
John J Koloedey
1121 Rosedale Ave
Wilmington DE 19809

Call Sign: K4YGG

Charles H Jordan Jr
4521 Roslyn Dr
Wilmington DE 19804

Call Sign: WA3UVR
Earl B Cummins
105 Rowland Park Blvd
Wilmington DE 19863

Call Sign: KB3AUC
Anna M Francisco
707 Rusina Dr
Wilmington DE 19809

Call Sign: WA0KRI
Roger O Beck
525 Ruxton Dr
Wilmington DE
198092869

Call Sign: KB3FQX
William A Rock Jr
536 Ruxton Dr
Wilmington DE 19809

Call Sign: K2WAR
William A Rock Jr
536 Ruxton Dr
Wilmington DE 19809

Call Sign: KA3ZIK
Cynthia A Francisco
707 Rysing Dr
Wilmington DE 19809

Call Sign: N3NIX
John D Francisco Sr
707 Rysing Dr
Wilmington DE 19809

Call Sign: N3NIY
Elizabeth M Francisco
707 Rysing Dr
Wilmington DE 19809

Call Sign: KB3VIB
Something Awful Amateur
Radio Society
323 S Cleveland Ave
Wilmington DE 19805

Call Sign: AG0ON
Something Awful Amateur
Radio Society
323 S Cleveland Ave
Wilmington DE 19805

Call Sign: KB3UXB
Brenden Mcneil
323 S Cleveland Ave
Wilmington DE 19805

Call Sign: W3VD
Brenden Mcneil
323 S Cleveland Ave
Wilmington DE 19805

Call Sign: WA3PTG
Harry T Hurst
302 S Clifton Ave
Wilmington DE 19805

Call Sign: KB3DDC
Miguel Pagan
111 S Jackson St
Wilmington DE 19805

Call Sign: KA3TKP
William Beacroft
21 S Pennewell Dr
Wilmington DE 19809

Call Sign: N9APS
Herbert L Schaaf Jr
3402 S Rockfield Dr
Wilmington DE 19810

Call Sign: KB3PZO
Erin M Murphy
431 S Sycamore St

Wilmington DE 19805

Call Sign: K3HAL
Harry A Lane
2507 Saint George St
Wilmington DE 19808

Call Sign: NY3Q
John F Pukalski Jr
2603 Salem Dr
Wilmington DE 19808

Call Sign: KB3QCV
Jeffrey E Stoklosa
254 Sandra Rd
Wilmington DE 19803

Call Sign: WB0JJX
Randall K Carlson
121 Scarborough Pk Dr
Apt 10
Wilmington DE 19804

Call Sign: N3OMP
William J Starkey
9 Servan Ct
Wilmington DE 19805

Call Sign: W3DNF
Joseph F Eberhart
702 Seville Ave
Wilmington DE 19809

Call Sign: KA3PTX
Edward J Delawski
1720 Shadybrook Rd
Wilmington DE 19803

Call Sign: KB3VZV
Gabriel J Bukowski
1820 Shalleross Ave
Wilmington DE 19806

Call Sign: N3MRX
Frank R Beverin

2638 Sherwood Dr
Wilmington DE 19808

Call Sign: KB3WOH
Paul L Lyseight Jr
2404 Silverside Rd
Wilmington DE 19810

Call Sign: W3JGY
Charles E Tee Jr
3315 Silverside Rd
Wilmington DE
198103306

Call Sign: N3TWE
Gary G Hoffer
3511 Silverside Rd
Wilmington DE
198023944

Call Sign: WB3KWF
Burton C Lodge
117 Silview Ave
Wilmington DE 19804

Call Sign: N3DEI
Michael L Seitelman
7 Smyrna Ave
Wilmington DE 19809

Call Sign: WG3O
Fred C Ingalls
108 Smyrna Ave
Wilmington DE 19809

Call Sign: N3FYA
Charles C Fifield
114 Somerset Rd
Wilmington DE 19808

Call Sign: K3DLX
Joseph L Olivere
801 Sonora Ave
Wilmington DE 19809

Call Sign: WA3VAI
Robert L Hills
122 Southwick Dr
Wilmington DE 19810

Call Sign: KA3DDL
Linda E Morgan
202 Spruce Ave
Wilmington DE
198042342

Call Sign: NM3X
Michael T Morgan
202 Spruce Ave
Wilmington DE
198042342

Call Sign: WA3CJG
Harry A Prosceno Jr
2308 St Francis St
Wilmington DE 19808

Call Sign: KB3UWU
Anatol N Oberhand
1306 Stanford Rd
Wilmington DE 19803

Call Sign: W3BSP
Roger B Proudfit
173 Steven Ln
Wilmington DE 19808

Call Sign: KG3E
Robert P Mc Caffrey
31 Stone Crop Rd
Wilmington DE
198101315

Call Sign: KB3KPR
Eugene T Pulcher
1612 Stoney Run Dr
Wilmington DE 19803

Call Sign: N3RND
Charles James Jr

205 Sunset Dr
Wilmington DE 19809

Call Sign: N3VLZ
Carol M James
205 Sunset Dr
Wilmington DE 19809

Call Sign: N3MRI
Carol M James
205 Sunset Dr
Wilmington DE 19809

Call Sign: WJ3E
Emilio Messina
1611 Sycamore St
Wilmington DE 19805

Call Sign: KB3GVV
Kameron J Houff
12 Talley Ct
Wilmington DE 19802

Call Sign: KB3MLR
Sherry W Burke
115 Talleysand Dr
Wilmington DE 19810

Call Sign: KB3HIB
Ermanno Dilorenzo
1016 Talon Ln
Wilmington DE
198071602

Call Sign: N3FWS
Ermanno Dilorenzo
1016 Talon Ln
Wilmington DE
198071602

Call Sign: KC3V
Ermanno Dilorenzo
1016 Talon Ln
Wilmington DE
198071602

Call Sign: N3GYL
James V Crescenzo
2617 Tanager Dr
Wilmington DE 19808

Call Sign: WA3RYH
Donald Eastburn
2710 Tanager Dr
Wilmington DE 19808

Call Sign: KC3YT
William E Willis
4517 Tarry Ln
Wilmington DE 19804

Call Sign: WB4ZEN
Paul J Weaver Jr
118 Tennessee Ave
Wilmington DE
198043510

Call Sign: KA3AAU
Guerrino J Mascelli Sr
2400 Thomas Ln
Wilmington DE 19810

Call Sign: KA3CDD
James M Hoffmann
4907 Threadneedle Rd
Wilmington DE
198072527

Call Sign: WA3AVD
Charles J Mc Gonigal
2518 Tigani Dr
Wilmington DE 19808

Call Sign: KA3LOV
Charles R Shisler
1004 Timberwyck Rd
Wilmington DE 19810

Call Sign: N3TMK
Stephen A Leishman

2603 Tonbridge Dr
Wilmington DE
198101216

Call Sign: N3ZGX
Douglas A Brunner
5 Vining Ln
Wilmington DE
198073127

Call Sign: W3FNI
Alfred J Maciejewski
1100 W 10th St
Wilmington DE 19806

Call Sign: WA8TKQ
William W Mosholder
2203 W 11th St
Wilmington DE 19805

Call Sign: N3QBG
Cortland K Steelman
501 W 11th St Ymca Rm
343
Wilmington DE 19801

Call Sign: KD3TX
George E Powell
2222 W 17th St
Wilmington DE 19806

Call Sign: NW3P
Alfred K Horn Jr
300 W 19th St
Wilmington DE
198024703

Call Sign: N3DNF
Elizabeth A Hansen
2602 W 19th St
Wilmington DE 19806

Call Sign: N3WKU
Nicholas D Caruso
909 W 21st St

Wilmington DE 19802

Call Sign: N3GEY
Albert J Haywood
805 W 22nd St
Wilmington DE
198023301

Call Sign: KA3AYZ
Cecilia R Haywood
805 W 22nd St
Wilmington DE 19802

Call Sign: K3VWP
Aaron Weissman
404 W 38th St
Wilmington DE 19802

Call Sign: N3YDA
Karissa D Hendershot
519 W 39th St
Wilmington DE
198022117

Call Sign: KB3GEK
Jachin D Spencer
1501 W 3rd St
Wilmington DE
198053507

Call Sign: KB3HYZ
Lesley A Suddard
4802 W Brigantine Ct
Wilmington DE 19808

Call Sign: KM3U
Irvin J Belasco
214 W Crest Rd
Wilmington DE 19803

Call Sign: N3JZB
Roger F Sund
103 W Holly Oak Rd
Wilmington DE 19809

Call Sign: W3ISO
Louis P Fournarakis
1607 W Newport Pike
Wilmington DE 19804

Call Sign: W3MZL
Fred W Hoover
206 W Pembrey Dr
Wilmington DE 19803

Call Sign: N3KSF
Jacob Earl Cummings Jr
402 W Summit Ave
Wilmington DE 19804

Call Sign: N3LEX
Clifford P Kendall
516 W Summit Ave
Wilmington DE
198041814

Call Sign: KB3FPP
Dennis L Waldorf
5605 W Timberview Ct
Wilmington DE 19808

Call Sign: N3EQK
Ronald L Rudinoff
1003 Wagoner Dr
Wilmington DE 19805

Call Sign: W3KOG
Nancy Y Palmer
11 Walnut Ridge Rd
Wilmington DE 19807

Call Sign: KB3RLH
Steven Macom
5504 Washington Blvd
Wilmington DE 19809

Call Sign: N2NJ
Anthony J Butterhof
111 Watford Rd W Gate
Farms

Wilmington DE 19808

Call Sign: KB3WKM
James D Tabor
4711 Weatherhill Dr
Wilmington DE 19808

Call Sign: N3LOE
Granville T Higgins
4847 Weatherhill Dr
Wilmington DE 19808

Call Sign: N3ALG
John K Hettler
1121 Webster Dr
Wilmington DE 19803

Call Sign: KB3VZU
John B Bolin II
1408 Wedgewood Rd
Wilmington DE 19805

Call Sign: KB3QVA
George O Lawton Jr
14 Weer Cir
Wilmington DE 19808

Call Sign: N8NA
Karl E Grunewald
4620 Weldin Rd
Wilmington DE
198034826

Call Sign: KB3UNP
Christopher C Chabalko
702 Westover Rd
Wilmington DE 19807

Call Sign: KA3TTV
Andrew J Ashton
2524 Wexford Dr
Wilmington DE 19810

Call Sign: N3GGA
Shraven K R Pakanati

11 Whitekirk Dr
Wilmington DE 19808

Call Sign: W3GKU
John G Obusek
3203 Whiteman Rd
Wilmington DE 19808

Call Sign: K3AS
Wilfred B Marsh
3216 Whiteman Rd
Wilmington DE
198082720

Call Sign: K3CVB
John J Lapasnick
2664 Whitman Dr
Wilmington DE 19808

Call Sign: W3MML
Howard O Morse
915 Wilson Rd
Wilmington DE 19803

Call Sign: KA3VLV
Timothy S Conrad
1013 Wilson Rd
Wilmington DE 19803

Call Sign: WA3UYJ
Albert R Pione
1611 Windybush Rd
Wilmington DE 19810

Call Sign: KB3KRJ
Christopher D Sanger
503 Wooddale Rd
Wilmington DE 19807

Call Sign: KB3KUI
John R Di Orio Jr
902 Woodland Ave
Wilmington DE 19808

Call Sign: WA1JZA

Dennis Mc Donald Jr
502 Woodland Dr
Wilmington DE 19809

Call Sign: KA3PXH
Louise M Lanahan
2100 Woodlawn Ave
Wilmington DE 19806

Call Sign: WA3PHT
James M Lanahan
2100 Woodlawn Ave
Wilmington DE 19806

Call Sign: K3FHG
Richard M Slutz
1015 Woodstream Dr
Wilmington DE 19810

Call Sign: W3BIY
Thomas J Hayes Jr
117 Wordsworth Dr
Wilmington DE
198082340

Call Sign: N3ZJX
Robert E Papp
12 Yale Rd
Wilmington DE 19808

Call Sign: K3AQ
Alexander E Papp
12 Yale Rd Cooper Farm
Wilmington DE
198082206

Call Sign: KA3VGK
Christine T Kavanagh
22 Yellow Pine Ct
Wilmington DE 19808

Call Sign: KA3UJJ
Hans Bigalke
1807 Zebley Rd
Wilmington DE 19810

Call Sign: K3COO
David L Ormond
Wilmington DE 19807

Call Sign: KT3R
Leslie E Sachau
Wilmington DE 19808

Call Sign: KA3VSP
Brian G Pasternak
Wilmington DE 19809

Call Sign: N3ZQC
Catherine E Burton
Wilmington DE 19809

Call Sign: W3HB
Howard M Berlin
Wilmington DE 19809

Call Sign: KE3QN
Edgar E Levingston
Wilmington DE 19899

Call Sign: N3YCG
Richard L Burton
Wilmington DE 19899

Call Sign: KB3IUM
Timothy N Joynes
Wilmington DE
198990132

FCC Amateur Radio License in Woodside

Call Sign: KB3CGA
Rene B Valladares
Woodside DE 199800233

Call Sign: KB3CGB
Dawn M Valladares
Woodside DE 199800233

FCC Amateur Radio License in Wyoming

Call Sign: N3KCB
Anthony L Clare
101 2nd St
Wyoming DE 19934

Call Sign: W3DBJ
Darryl B Jones
101 2nd St
Wyoming DE 19934

Call Sign: KA3LNA
Jay G Lewis
Box 360A
Wyoming DE 19934

Call Sign: KB3PRK
Stephanie K Dunn
162 Downey Oak Cir
Wyoming DE 19934

Call Sign: N3ZCA
Paul W Cable
39 Front St
Wyoming DE 19934

Call Sign: KB3FWB
Benjamin R Kneisley
4508 Mud Mill Rd
Wyoming DE 19934

Call Sign: KB3LJC
Samuel R Johnson
10 N Railroad Ave
Wyoming DE 19934

Call Sign: KB3QCP
Douglas A George
1125 Tower Rd
Wyoming DE 19934

Call Sign: KB3QPH
J Brian Diaz

Wyoming DE 19934

**FCC Amateur Radio
License in Yorklyn**

Call Sign: N3JCW
Robert H Palmatary Jr
Yorklyn DE 19736

www.ingramcontent.com/pod-product-compliance
Lightning Source LLC
Chambersburg PA
CBHW082134290526
45794CB00008B/3033